Our Faith Adventure

by
Kay D. Pierce

authorHOUSE®

AuthorHouse™
1663 Liberty Drive, Suite 200
Bloomington, IN 47403
www.authorhouse.com
Phone: 1-800-839-8640

First published by AuthorHouse 10/8/2008

ISBN: 978-1-4343-9600-6 (sc)

Library of Congress Control Number: 2008905397

Printed in the United States of America
Bloomington, Indiana

This book is printed on acid-free paper.

*Unless otherwise indicated, Bible quotations are taken from New King James Version
of the Bible, The Inspirational Study Bible.*

Capitalized in reverences to God His and Him

I dedicate this book to my husband Ray for his encouragement.

My children Stacy, Carroll, Chris, Detra, Justin, Joshua, Jonathan, Michael, Sarah, and Rebecca; my life would not be the same without your love and support.

Also to my grandchildren Tiffany, Faith, Hope, MaKenzie, Leah, Shayla and Jordan

TABLE OF CONTENTS

CHAPTER 1

FIELD OF DAISIES

If you could have anything in the world, what would you ask for? I was surprised when God ask me that question again and again. When I began to focus on what was missing in my life. It brought me to a new awareness that there had to be more and I wanted it for my life. There was only one answer for me to give. I knew a closer walk with God was what I wanted for my life!

I drifted off to sleep and upon awakening, realized that I was in the in the middle of a field surrounded by millions of daises blowing in the gentle breeze. The plush green field of new grass looked too perfect to be real. Surrounding me, in every direction as far as my eyes could see, were trillions of flowers. The beauty of it was breathtaking I wondered could this be a dream?

How could this be a dream when it looks so real? The bright rays of the brilliant morning sun overhead were piercing through the clouds and blinding me. I wondered how did I get here. I knew it was God who had transported me there. Somehow I knew this was the beginning of my adventure, the voyage that God was going to use to draw me closer to Him and literally transform my life forever.

My life had plenty of problems (weeds, I like to call them) that were holding me captive. Not only were they choking the life out of my flowers, my life wasn't all that it could be. The problems that I faced daily had consumed me. I was constantly focused on dealing with my problems and I took little time to be thankful for the good things in my life. Isn't that human nature?

We concentrate on all the things that are going wrong and easily forget about everything that is going well. We have to decide what we'll dwell on the good or the bad. I knew I needed to slow down, taking time to enjoy life's simple pleasures. But who doesn't these days? I thought about the question God had asked me. I decided to get going and begin my spiritual journey.

That's when I noticed all these weeds tangled around my feet. They were holding me captive and would soon be choking the life out of my beautiful flowers. I tried to break loose of their hold. Carefully and with much effort, I untangled enough of them so I could stand. God began to show me that the weeds represented all the cares of this world and the daisies all of God's blessings.

I know my life is in God's hand, yet I'm not enjoying all that God has blessed me with. I want to be so close that I give the Lord total management over every area of my life. I wondered, how do I change? With only myself to rely on, it would be impossible. Yet, I trusted the Holy Spirit to lead me, on this grand journey. Somehow I knew this was the beginning of the transformation that would ultimately change me from the inside out.

Realizing the sin that I was in bondage to I knelt down to pray.

"God, please forgive me for trying to manage my own life. My will be done replaced Thy will be done, I'm guilty of idolatry because you weren't first in my life. Forgive me for dwelling on all the things wrong in my life, instead of looking at all my blessings. Forgive me, Father, for having an agenda that didn't allow me enough time to spend alone with you. Release me and let me live for you. Amen.

The sun didn't blind me as I opened my eyes and I looked down at my feet, I saw green grass where the weeds had been. One other thing that I noticed is that I was facing the opposite direction. Following God means we pray about everything that's bothering us, especially those situations where it isn't evident to us what we should do. We give everything each day to our Father as a package. We know only He can unravel and take care of all the pieces. If He's holding our problems it frees us up to enjoy our lives.

The Bible states in Matthew 11:28-30, "Come to me, all you who are weary and burdened, and I will give you rest. Take my yoke upon you and learn from me, for I am gentle and humble in heart, and you will find rest for your souls. For my yoke is easy, and my burden light." (NIV) He never meant for us to carry the weight of the world on our shoulders.

My life is far from being problem free. Yet I know God is in control. He has taken me through many things that I couldn't handle alone. Learning to allow Him to manage my life cost me very little and the benefits I gained are plenty.

It reminds me of the Serenity Prayer: "God grant me the serenity to accept the things I cannot change, the Courage to change the things I can, and Wisdom to know the difference." But there is no peace unless you realize God is in control and some things we are unable to change. You can worry or you can pray and rely on a higher power.

If I'd written that poem I would have added this line. God, help me to bask in your presence always, serving you first and never taking you for granted.

There are many challenges we face, but whom we allow into our lives to help us that makes the difference.

The Bible states I can do all things through Jesus Christ, who strengthens me. (Phil. 4:13)

My life is far from being free of problems, yet I know God is still in charge. He has never taken me through something that I couldn't handle with His help. The answer is to focus on my creator and allowing Him management of my life.

God loves us and desires our attention. As we focus on Him we'll be blessed with joy. Faith takes over, and we live joyfully unencumbered because we know God's blessings are all around us. Someday Jesus will call my name. He could ask me how much of my life I gave to Him. We all have a choice to make. Follow our own desires (our will) or do the will of our Father, giving ourselves completely to God.

We all know the story of the rich young ruler found in Mark 10: 17- 21, who asked Jesus how to be saved. Jesus said, "You shall not murder,' 'You shall not commit adultery,' 'You shall not steal,' 'You shall not bear false witness,' 'Honor your father and your mother,' and 'You shall love your neighbor as yourself."

The young man said to Him, "All these things I have kept from my youth. What do I still lack? Jesus said to him, "If you want to be perfect, go, sell what you have, and give to the poor, and you will have treasure in heaven; and come follow me."

The young man had wanted to know what he had to do. Jesus told him, "Come follow me, but first sell everything you have and give it to the poor." The young man wanted eternal life but was unwilling to pay the price. Jesus recognized the problem was not one of disobeying the commandments but rather putting wealth in front of God.

Jesus needs followers who can keep up with Him and aren't bogged down with something they should have given up. Riches can weigh you down, making you lag behind, if they take priority.

Nothing should come between your getting close and following Jesus.

That rich young ruler's eyes were on his riches. He may have thought a donation would be all he needed to give, but Jesus asked him to give everything. He was a good man who kept six of the commandments. Yet, a sinner breaking all those has a better chance for eternity if he repents and gives everything he has to follow Jesus. What are you willing to pay?

The question we must ask ourselves: " Is whether there's anything you are unwilling to give to God if He asks?" When we look back at our lives, I believe we'll be able to see all of our accomplishments: the mountains we climbed, tragedies we made it through, valleys we've forged because of our great faith. It takes **Faith** to move mountains. We draw our strength from God and only through our strength in God was it possible.

When I meet God face to face; will He call my name? Hopefully God will say, "Everything I had planned for you to do was done; enter my good and faithful one." Pastor Carl Morris preached on this subject last night. Some day Jesus will call your name. He could ask you, what percentage of your life did you give to Him? What will your answer be?

The journey isn't judged by how quickly you get to where you are going, but by how many seeds you plant and people's lives you changed along the way. Last Sunday at our church, Abundant Life, Michael Murray spoke. The thing that I remember the most is that our motive really matters. Two people could both be doing the same job, voluntarily cleaning up their church. When these two men stand before God they will be asked, "What did you do for Jesus?"

The first one said, "I cleaned the church every week!" God's reply was, "Why did you do that?" Puzzled by the question, the man thought about it. He was honest and said "I did it for all the praises I got from others." All his works were burned up like straw and stubble. He still got to enter into heaven, but had done nothing in his lifetime for the Master.

The second man stands before the Lord and is asked, "What did you do for me?" He said, "I cleaned the church each week, Lord." Again the Lord looks at him and asks, "Why?" "Well, our church didn't have an abundance of people or money. I knew the money would go much farther if I did a job we would normally have to hire done." "Well done," says Jesus. "The work you did was done as unto the Lord so your work can't be burned up, it is solid gold. Enter in, my faithful one.

Although both men did the same job, the motive is what made the difference. Tears streamed down my face. I could think of some times when I had started out with the right motive. Later, as things got rough, I wondered what is in this for me. The same work when done with the wrong motive will all be in vain.

Standing in that field of daisies blowing in the gentle breeze, I was lost, unsure of which path to follow. I cuffed my hand, over my eyes, to shield the brilliant rays of sunshine from blinding me. The awesome fragrance of the flowers and the hot sun beating down on me only added to the daze I was already in. Struggling to get in control, I realized I had to relinquish control.

This time I was going to wait patiently, allowing God to lead me. I squinted, looking in every direction. I was searching for my guide. Only God knew which way I should go. Only after giving up did I hear a still small voice leading me one step at a time, finding my way with the help of the Holy Spirit to the edge of the field of flowers. Just ahead was a clearing. As the journey begins I allow God to lead me. Yet, I haven't turned all my problems over to Him. Some of the weeds are still tangled up around my feet, making every step a struggle.

The weeds are my problems: their by products are stress, discontentment, lack of peace, and many others. Stress makes it hard for me to think and act like I should. Under major stress no one would recognize me as a born-again Christian. My behavior even surprises me. My stress seems to happen when there are too many things or events happening at the same time.

Stress is a part of every one's life and there isn't a way to totally remove it. I have heard that we have good stress and bad stress. It doesn't matter of which kind you have. Too much stress is unhealthy for us. In my past too much stress caused me to lie awake at night worrying. Since things never did happen in life how I imagined, worry held no benefits.

I learned by reading God's word that worry was the opposite of faith. Worry just never seemed to have any payoff. God didn't make my stress go away or give me only good stress. With God leading me that stress no longer eats from the inside out. Faith in Him causes us to focus on the one with the solution, God. Knowing He has the answer to our problems relieves the heavy load.

I was getting ready for the journey of a lifetime. There was an avalanche up ahead full of more problems and more stress than I had ever experienced at the same time. Only I didn't know that. God was strengthening me as I drew closer, preparing me for my quest.

When I tried to live a Christian life without following God's plan it was overwhelming. He never meant for it to work that way. Kevin Baird told us that as we go through this life God will let us go through **Faith** adventures. The things we will encounter will be so rough that we must rely on God. He wants us to remember that we couldn't make it without Him. If we are in control, we will not be victorious.

God offers us the perfect plan if we lean 100% on Him. "For God so loved the world that He gave His one and only Son." Jesus died so that we could live. First, we give Him our hearts. When we ask Him to forgive us for all our sins He does. Later Jesus becomes our advocate to the Father. Anything we pray for we should always ask for in Jesus' name.

That seems to be the easier part. Next, we learn we must die to our own self-will and live for Jesus. My life is no longer my own. Every day I'm faced with the same temptations. Will I give up willingly what I want to do and allow God to chart my activities?

Seeking God for the answers will lighten our load. The person who leans on the Master is no longer leaning on self or others for additional support or power. That person looks to the Savior for victories over everything. Even if we fail God will turn our mistakes around for our good. God will turn everything around for those who seek the Lord with all their heart. The Bible states in Psalms 55:22, "Cast your burden on the Lord, and He shall sustain you; He shall never permit the righteous to be moved."

Things don't bother the person leaning on Jesus. Worry is replaced with faith. We trust not in our ability but Christ's ability to work through us. There is nothing too hard for God or us when Jesus is living in us. Stress becomes opportunities for others to see Jesus in us.

Major stress provides us with many more opportunities for our faith to grow as we witness to others. As we grow in the Lord, God will cushion us so the effects of stress are barely felt. I shouldn't be amazed by my lack of stress. Daily I give all my problems to Him. We walk through life together. I remember it's not me, but Him working through me that makes all things possible. The plan is so easy I wonder why I tried so long to do things my way.

CHAPTER 2

EXCESS BAGGAGE

Suddenly, I noticed this huge black bag lying on the ground just ahead of me. What was it doing here and why was my name written on it? I figured it must be for the trip I'd be making. But I soon realized this bag had always been there at my side though I'd never been able to see it before. It also proved to be much heavier than it looked.

What's in here anyway, I wondered? I was focusing on the weight of the bag I'd have to lug everywhere. Do I really need all this stuff for my journey? It must have weighed over 100 pounds. So when I looked inside, I discovered.

The spirit of rejection was in that heavy black bag, weighing it down. As I attempted to pick it up, I realized that locked deep inside me were the emotional scars of a lifetime. Over the years I had collected these hurts one by one and held on to them tightly like trophies. Little did I know that they were my hidden treasures, concealed deep inside myself. They affected every relationship I had. So many of my choices in life were made out of a fear of not being accepted. Many times while growing up I felt rejected and alone never really knowing what I did or failed to do.

Out of every tragedy, God will take the ashes and use them as ointment to heal our wounds. God used a devastating ordeal in my life, back in 1992, to begin the healing process. Reflecting back, I remember it was the time that I had just finished all my college courses except one, student teaching. I sat in the college library while all the students, including myself, were given their placements. Some were elated because they were placed in the grade they had always wanted, others excited because they were at one of the best schools.

For me there was nothing to be excited about. First, I was very reluctant to accept the fact that I had been given fifth grade. But that wasn't the end of it. The school had a reputation for being one of the roughest schools in the city. As I left the building, I recalled what God had spoken to me only moments earlier. You will not like your placement but it will turn out for your good.

The first day of student teaching went okay as far as I could tell. I was taken on a tour of the building and introduced to the teacher I would be working with. She took no time to show me a stack of papers I could grade. I was busy and very bored at the same time.

The incident that remains most in my mind, although there are many that I could share, is the day it started to snow. Now we are living in South Carolina and snow in this part of the state is rare. These fifth graders wanted to go outside to have fun. The excitement could not be contained and to add to that over the loudspeaker it was announced that there would be an early dismissal.

The cafeteria would serve lunch but each class would file down and pick up their lunches, returning to their classrooms to eat. That way the entire school could eat at the same time. Miss L told me to stay with the class while she went somewhere. I have to admit I was concerned about getting my homemade lunch heated up. All the microwaves were in the cafeteria.

When someone came along passing out milk, I asked her if she minded watching the class for a few minutes while I went down to heat up my food. I didn't get halfway down the hall when Miss L spotted me coming toward her. Her eyes got as big as golf balls! "You didn't leave the class unattended, did you?" she spoke sharply. My response was no, but the tone of my voice showed that I felt undignified that she thought I could have been that stupid.

As I left early that day, with no ride, I can still remember walking across the white snowy field with tears streaming down my face. The feelings of being rejected and alone surfaced again after all these years. What about my dream and God's promise this was supposed to turn out for my good, but how?

There were many other incidents, but the bottom line was it only took Miss L a few weeks to convince me that I wasn't just an inexperienced novice, but was actually too stupid to teach. It only got worse. Instead of teaching me what I needed to know and helping me, she criticized me constantly. Later it was Miss L that ran to my student teaching advisor to tell her I had problems. In the end, the college pulled me out of student teaching, unsure of what the actual problem was.

The rejection and humiliation caused a metamorphic change in me. I was filled with self-pity and doubts. The dream I had of becoming a teacher was out of my grasp. I questioned whether or not I was cut out to be a teacher. My husband saw the joy literally sucked out of me. I was miserable, totally void of my usual happy nature. Fear had gripped me and my confidence was replaced with a sense of failure.

I hope none of you have experienced such emotional pain. I felt that my dream, my passion was crumbling center-stage for everyone to see. I was so distraught that I couldn't coherently read my Bible. I held it close, that day I had been called to come into the dean's office to talk to her about what they were going to do.

Two little slips of paper with typed scriptures on them fell into my lap. As I read those two verses I found it was just what I needed. With that glimmer of hope, I went to meet the dean. I held on desperately to God's word and His promise that He held my future in His hands.

I sat in the dean's office and immediately I knew God was working on my behalf. Our pastor had been praying that the dean wouldn't be able to sleep until she made the right choice. Her first statement to me was, "You don't know how I've tossed back and forth last night trying to decide what to do," she stated.

In the end, I was given a new placement, but not to finish my student teaching. Because too many weeks had passed, making it impossible. It was great being in a school where I was praised and encouraged. The teacher was up for a Disney award for excellence and I can see why. It was a wonderful experience and I loved the classes. He had enough confidence in me to allow me to teach the six grade Social Studies class. With everything going for me my self-confidence gradually returned.

On the negative side, I had to face the graduating students who were leaving me behind. How would I face them? First, there were the stares everyone gave me as I walked into a room. Everyone knew that I wouldn't be graduating and why.

Yet, that new position turned out to be the best thing to happen to me. God gave me inner strength and courage. When I ran into classmates, I was so excited to tell them what a wonderful experience I had. The looks on their faces were astounding. That placement gave me the hands-on experience I needed. The new teacher believed in me and I realized that no one could kill your dreams unless you give up.

I started examining the contents of my bag again. Rejection, I was all too familiar with that. As I picked it up, I realized how ridiculous it was to hold on to it any longer. I had made it through one of the worst times in my life and the rejection didn't phase me any longer. It eventually allowed me to grow and see myself from the Master's eyes.

I allowed God to reveal the rejection. One by one I prayed and forgave all those who had hurt me. Rejection could have held me captive; instead God delivered me. How did I let go of them? By praying to forgive all those who had shamed me. God healed me emotionally so I could begin again.

Second, when I did return the next semester to redo my student teaching, it was the whispering that caught my eye. Those words didn't carry the venom as before. I was shielded by my faith in God. The words bounced off me like bullets would off of a bulletproof vest.

What should have normally torn me apart became a praise report. It was a minor nuisance, yet I held my head up high, knowing God was working everything out for my good. I had Him to thank for the wonderful teaching experience where I gained confidence and support. The stares and the whispering didn't bother me anymore because I had grown stronger in the Lord. He totally healed my wounds of rejection.

With my new-found confidence, I held my head up high. I was now ready. This time I was placed in second grade and at the best school. Everyone was amazed at how well I handled everything. Many of my classmates told me they couldn't have done what I did. What started out as disgrace, ended up being a commendation.

No one knew the pain I had once carried on the inside. The devil really used the hurts against me, because in the past I had refused to turn them over to God. Those painful experiences had crushed my self-esteem and left behind ugly scars. Words have the ability to give life or death. It was time for healing.

God changed my inner core to be His child and be proud of everything we could accomplish together. I held my head up high when I received my diploma. God worked everything out in a way I never would have chosen. He allowed this experience to begin to heal my spirit of rejection. The world can hate me! Yet, God's love is enough to see me through.

CHAPTER 3

THE GRAVE

I began looking in my bag again. This time I found my unwillingness to forgive others. What is this doing in my bag? There has to be a mistake, I thought. Who haven't I forgiven, Lord? Sometimes we store our hurts deep inside and bury them so deep within us that we forget that they are even there.

God remembers and works on us until we are ready to let go of the offense. I don't even know the day my physical pain began or what I thought was the cause of it. I do remember that the pain was in my hip joints. Since I sleep on my side it became difficult. The pain would be gone for days and then be aggravated by walking on uneven surfaces, being on my feet too much, or holding my daughter on my lap.

I spent many days wanting to be free and this agony. My doctor thought it was arthritis. I didn't think so, because it came and went. After about a year I met someone at a birthday party I attended with my youngest child. She recommended that I try physical therapy. At that point I was ready to try anything. The physical therapist had helped people who were in far worse shape than I, due to car accidents.

I needed a referral from my doctor. I had to make several appointments with him following up on my case before he would refer me. I even went to a neighboring town for the last office visit. I was determined I wasn't leaving his office without that slip of paper. I called and scheduled the appointment for physical therapy.

The day arrived and I was ready. I arrived at the hospital in plenty of time to get to the right place. I found the waiting room and went in. I was asked, by the receptionist, "Did you register two doors down and on the right?" " No one told me I had to go there first," I replied. What they said next angered me. I would probably miss my appointment today because of the paperwork that I needed to do.

I was beginning to think that every step I took forward caught me by surprise. I had to turn around and go back. Eventually I did get to see the physical therapist, she was very busy, and I waited what seemed like hours for my turn. She was very nice and I explained the problems I was experiencing. It only took her minutes to figure out the problem. My right hip was coming in and out of its socket. She showed me the exercises I would need to do in order to strengthen those muscles that hold the bones in place. Also I was shown how to pop my hipbone back in place.

Months earlier I had woken up in excruciating pain. I went downstairs to sit on the couch so I wouldn't wake my husband. "God," I thought, "why am I in this much pain? I would do anything for the pain to stop." I thought I have prayed to be healed. Why hasn't God answered? Lack of forgiveness is one reason that will block your requests from being answered. Lord, is there someone I haven't forgiven? At that moment two faces flashed in my mind, my mom and dad. I really thought that I had all that behind me.

I prayed immediately. Then I ask God, what do you want me to do? What does the Bible say to do? Confess your sins and God will be faithful to forgive you. I did that, I thought, and go to the one you have offended, asking for his forgiveness. God was asking me to go to my parents and ask for their forgiveness. They live three states away. We had a trip planned in a few weeks. God's timing is always perfect!

At my dad's home I got him alone and asked him to forgive me for any pain or grief I'd put him through when I was growing up. He replied, "I probably wasn't the easiest person to live with either."

Mom, on the other hand, was so excited to see me that I was never able to ask her. Even when we went out to lunch, she never stopped talking. I left with a sense of dissatisfaction, but tried to let myself off the hook, thinking, God understands I tried. Months later, I felt compelled to call her and I asked her to forgive me over the phone.

Standing in the field of daisies, swaying in the gentle breeze I began to pray. God, I want to forgive my mom for all the hurts I hold inside. Scene after scene ran before my closed eyes, revealing time after time when a hurt was stored deep inside. Praying, forgiving, and letting go were all I needed to do. I gave up everything to free myself so that I could live.

God put me in the right place to get physically stronger. Forgiveness was dealt with and love was dwelling in my heart. With everything in place, God healed me. What I remember most is sitting on that couch. One moment in agony, crying out to God, and wondering why He was allowing me to suffer. Later, thanking God for the pain that helped me run back into His arms again.

I took a deep breath and noticed such a wonderful feeling of peace and tranquility. With all those burdens lifted I felt light as a feather. There was no longer the confusion I had experienced earlier. I felt confident in my ability to hear clearly. Now, I was relying on the Holy Spirit to lead me.

As I allowed God to lead me where He wanted me to go, I knew I had to give my life completely to Him, holding nothing back. "Lord, what about all these problems?" I asked. His answer was so simple. He said, "Just keep your eyes on me and I'll take care of them."

Wow! I felt the weight of worry, lack of forgiveness, and all my problems fall to the ground. There is no place for these when God takes our hand to lead us. He should carry it all. This journey would take twice as long carrying around those heavy burdens. The weight of all that stuff weighs a person down. Now, in my life all the problems and burdens became light as feathers.

Only after giving up did I hear a still small voice leading me one step at a time, finding my way with the help of the Holy Spirit to the edge of the field of flowers. Just ahead was a ravine. While I was being healed, I opened my bag and pulled out rejection and unwillingness to forgive. There was no room for these things to weigh my life down any longer.

The ravine below was a good place for these to go. As for the stone of an unwillingness to forgive, it was very heavy but with God's help we managed to heave it over the side. Wow, it broke into a million pieces! The feeling was indescribable! Taking in a deep breath I sighed, free at last. Wonderful or marvelous wouldn't begin to describe how spectacular I felt! For the first time in my life, I knew I was worthy of God's love.

We must depend on God for our acceptance and approval. I couldn't make others want to get to know me or want to spend time with me. When you look into the mirror you see your reflection or the image of your physical body. The mirror doesn't reflect your needs, desires, and wants. How then can people tell what it is you want? Only God knows us and accepts us just as we are.

In the spirit realm, I'm standing at the edge of the ravine. I have put my complete trust in God. I'm walking back to that spectacular field of yellow, pink and blue daisies. While standing in the middle of that field, I decided to pray. I definitely knew I couldn't go back to my life that was so void of God. I ask for Jesus to lead me. I want to follow God's plan and let His will become mine. I opened my eyes, amazed to see only flowers at my feet. My life was no longer tangled up in all those weeds.

There are mountains just ahead. I check to see that I have everything I need for the climb. I have the word of God to stand on and the Holy Spirit to guide my footsteps. When I begin to pray, the Holy Spirit whispers; "If you will allow me to lead you, then you won't have to be a slave again to fear." I'm no longer afraid. I pray, asking God for the strength needed for this journey. I will not be fooled again, thinking I don't need God because it looks like such an easy climb.

CHAPTER 4

AVALANCHIE

Everyone has been there, when everything seems to be going wrong and even those things that are going right are overlooked in the middle of your crisis. Problems come tumbling down and life is so chaotic. We feel the weight of the boulders burdening us with more difficulties than it seems possible to handle. There appears to be no easy solutions. You are having what I call an "avalanche experience."

Now, in the spirit, overhead I see rocks tumbling down the mountain headed for me. I run for cover, realizing nothing matters now except staying alive. Will my problems bury me at the foot of this mountain? Earlier, I had tried to get a clear head and I prayed. What does God want me to do next? I just want to survive this rockslide.

My avalanche experience began on January 11, when I had a simple surgical procedure done to find out what was wrong. I never fully recovered. Oh, I woke up all right and my husband drove me home from the hospital. But the pain had become constant. The doctor had said three days of rest then everything would be back to normal. Only it wasn't days turned into weeks, and I was in even more hours of pain than before I had the procedure done. I spent countless days in agony wondering, was I ever going to recover? I was unable to do any of my usual activities. My days were spent sitting, resting in bed, or watching television. Although it may have been an attack of the enemy, I failed to recognize what it was.

Anything we go through is also a test of our faith. Who held the solution? God had strengthened me, drawn me so close, and rekindled the fire that burned bright for the love I had for Him. Prayer and reading the Bible had strengthened my faith. Was I upset that I was going through this? I sure was! The avalanche brought more problems than I could deal with at one time. But God was taking me on a walk of FAITH, only by depending on Him could I survive. I needed Father God to rescue me and help me through the problems one step at a time.

In my eyes it didn't look very good in both the natural and the spirit. Although I knew that if I died I'd see my Master face to face, I didn't want to die! Running as fast as my physically out-of-shape legs could go; the very hand of God led me into a cave at the base of this huge mountain. Safe for now and all alone, I need time to think. God made a way for me, when there wasn't one that I could see. I'm lost from this world and all alone. I'm in a cave where the presence of God hovers. This is an answer to one of my prayers, to feel His presence.

Reflecting back to what happened after having the procedure, I was left wondering the reason for all this suffering. So I telephoned the doctor and she explained the results of the tests done in outpatient surgery. The pathologist recommended a complete hysterectomy based on the observation of the ovary. It looked suspicious, maybe cancer. God, don't let me die I thought. The doctor told me I needed a major operation, so I agreed to have the operation. We set the date over the phone for as soon as possible, about two weeks away.

CHAPTER 5

THE CAVE

There was nothing to distract me from spending time with God. So utterly alone cut off from the entire world. Yet not really alone at all, I am with my Savior. I am depending on Him to be there. If I'm going to get out of this cave alive. God was using everything I was going through for my good. On the positive side, my faith grew, as I turned to God for help. Days went by and while I was still in pain, I had to forget what I had planned and depend on God no matter what happened. In any bad experience we can still have a positive attitude. Looking to God was easier because I believed He held the answers for my life. He'll have to show me the way. I rely on Him more and more each day. God is my only chance for survival. Whether my final outcome is to live or to die, God is in control, and I look to Him for direction. I must walk in His love, relying on His strength.

In the past, I was so busy taking care of business. Yet, now God is my only business. Getting out of this cave alive is not as important as how I spend the time inside with God. Through this trial, I grow closer to my Creator. I began looking back and wishing that I was in the middle of those daises again. The past problems seem so trite compared to this life-and-death situation.

Well, God was who brought me through that experience. Just like an avalanche where we are loaded down with rocks. The opposite is also true. Daily our God loads us down with more blessings than we realize. The daisies represented all of God's blessings in our lives. All these rocks, symbolic of my burdens, have taken me captive.

Right now covered with this avalanche God's goodness is impossible to see with my natural eyes. Yet, my spirit man knows that God's love never stops blessing me. I don't have to see it to know that it is there but every inch of me feels his goodness. He has plans to prosper me, not to harm me.

Right now with all my pain and physicals problems, complaining seems natural. I want to complain and that would seem like the thing to do to tell it how it is. Yet, my spirit man knows that words temper how we feel. If we feel bad, complaining will only make us feel worse. Yet, God is the only one that will hear me. In fact He hears all my complaints, even those unspoken ones I hold in my heart. Complaining focuses our attention on what we lack or don't have and as a result we alienate ourselves from God.

What I really wanted was a closer relationship with our Lord. This situation has forced me to make a choice. The only one who will help me is the one that will draw me closer to God. In the past I had neglected to spend time in God's word to cultivate our relationship. The devil loves it when we do our thing instead of God's.

Whose report would I believe, man's or God's? On the following Wednesday night at church, Pastor Carl, preached on faith. It wasn't just a sermon, it was life changing. He talked about going to the store to purchase an item. If we have enough money in our account we can buy it. He paralleled it with our faith account. When we need faith to believe for a rescue from a cave, we need enough faith in our account. When we pray, we receive it.

After hearing that sermon, I felt very strongly in my heart that I couldn't go through with the surgery. I had enough faith to believe God for the healing that I needed. Let me add God can heal us anyway He wants to. Sometimes he uses doctors and operations to heal us. In this case, I felt in my heart that God would heal me if I'd only give Him the chance.

Faith rose up even higher in me, as I believed God for a miracle. Just as I stood up at the end of that Wednesday night service, tears were trickling down my face. Faith rose up in me, giving me the strength I needed to heave a huge boulder off. Thank you, God; I have the faith to believe you can rescue me.

That night at home, the Holy Spirit spoke to me, saying, "Whom are you going to follow, man or me?" Whom are you going to follow? Those words echoed through my ears. I listened and waited for God to lead me out of the cave. I closed my eyes and when I opened them, I saw a light piercing the darkness. I walked slowly in the direction from where it came.

The Holy Spirit asked me to be sure to listen to the CD on healing the next day and meditate on it. I might add that I had listened to it several times before. I had purchased the CD from Robb and Shanda Tripp. It was Bible scriptures on healing read by Shanda with background music.

I drifted off to sleep, listening to the scriptures on healing, waiting for tomorrow. The very next day I dropped two of our children off at school. I decided to go on to the Wal-Mart store for necessities. I was pushing my buggy or shopping cart through the store, when nature called and I knew I had to use the restroom. I had a bowel movement, I was so overjoyed because it was very large and I had been constipated for over two weeks.

I thought to myself, I wish every system of my body worked to such perfection. The Holy Spirit spoke to me and said it does. Well, I went straight home and listened to the scriptures on that CD. I closed my eyes and meditated, giving it my full attention. I felt the touch of the Holy Spirit. I knew that what I had just experienced was God's healing touch. It was a knowing in my innermost being that healing was taking place at that very moment in time.

It happened right after I had listened to the scripture about the woman with an issue of blood. She had touched the hem of Jesus' clothing and knew immediately that she was healed. I thought to myself, Lord, that's just like me, and this female problem that has gone on for eleven years. That woman had such faith that day. Jesus asked his disciples "Who touched me." That same healing power is available to everyone today. I knew without any doubt healing was taking place in my body. Then I heard a still small whisper say, "Call Diane." I went to call a Christian friend of mine.

I wanted to tell her I wasn't going to have the operation because I was healed. She was so excited and said, "That's the best news I've heard all day." We talked for a while when she said, "Well, that's just like the woman that touched the hem of Jesus' garment." That was the confirmation I needed, because only God knew how I related to that particular scripture.

You may feel dead tired yet watch how quickly we scramble to our feet to be set free. The rocks were heavy but I managed to roll them out of the way one by one. Thank you for the strength that was not in me, but in you, Lord. Wiggling through the hole, I was out of that cave, free again. Wow! I jumped for joy, knowing God had healed me. It was what I had prayed for, more importantly it was what I stood in faith for. Believing in God's ability to do whatever we ask according to His will. I continued on my climb up the huge mountain!

CHAPTER 6

THE MOUNTAIN CLIMB

I said goodbye to my friend Diane and heard the Holy Spirit say, "It will only get harder the longer you wait." I knew I had to make the phone call to let the doctor know I wasn't having the surgery. I dialed the number and took a deep breath. Why was it so hard to do? Would the doctor understand? No, I didn't think she would. I tried to explain to the nurse that I wouldn't be having the surgery. After speaking to a nurse from the doctor's office I hung up the phone. It was then that I realized the pain had returned. So I went to lie down.

It always seems like a huge emotional challenge to obey the Holy Spirit because I'm faced with doing things I don't always want to do. Sometimes, I feel a willingness to obey, but not at this time. Yet, when I obey, what I have noticed is that things always turn out better than I could have imagined and I feel well inside.

Being led by the Holy Spirit is one of the greatest adventures of my life, and at time, one of the hardest. Right now I have peace, although this is the hardest thing God has ever asked me to do, or so it seems. God loves me so much that he places me in situations where I will have to grow into a giant woman of God. As a warrior I need the courage from Jesus, the strengthening from God, and the protection of my guardian angels.

I have never regretted following God's advice. I would never attempt some of the things God has led me to do. I'm climbing higher and higher up the side of this rather large mountain, never knowing when I'll reach the top or how many more mountains I will have to climb.

Daily, I stood on the promise of my healing. Did I feel healed? It wasn't how I felt that really mattered. I relied not on my senses but on the word of God. Honestly, feelings have very little to do with it. My feelings didn't heal me, God did. Yes, I was healed and it was a process that in my case took months and months. Even in the Bible Jesus healed people in many different ways; He never sent anyone away. We want an instant miracle with proof to see and feel the results immediately.

> **FAITH** believes in the unseen,
> **HOPES** in the impossible, and
> **LOVES** at all times.

Love, even in the midst of your crisis. Don't take your eyes off Christ and you'll receive your miracle. We want to be healed instantly and feel great immediately; but do we spend the time getting to know the Healer? Or are eyes just on receiving the gift of healing? That doesn't require very much of us, just the faith to believe. God gives; we receive: and go on our way. Yet it is the gift that should cause a transformation on the inside of our hearts. God also deposits **LOVE** into our **Faith** account. It may seem that nothing is different, yet everything is.

It is through adversity that we grow closer to God, little else matters. If we get that right, everything else will get worked out.

God is for us, not against us, and in those tough times we must remain strong, growing and going on to do His will. How do we do our part? We stand firm, believing God's word not man's. The doctors may even tell us it is hopeless. But whose report will you believe? The thing to do is rely on a higher power to see you through, starting with prayer. We must hang on to our **HOPE** and **FAITH** that sees the impossible become possible through God.

God has a healing plan custom made just for you and as we close our eyes to what seems like reality and we open them to God's plan, it will happen. I do know it was His plan to heal me! I'm waiting for the adventure to continue…

THERE ARE STILL MANY MOUNTAINS TO CLIMB.

Four weeks after the procedure, my husband Ray and I return to the doctors for a follow-up appointment. My husband asked if I was bringing him along for support. When our faith is weak, other Christians can help us. I wanted him present when the doctors discussed the evidence and why she thought I needed an operation. The doctor still didn't know that I had canceled the operation. Rather, she thought that I was going to reschedule it.

The evidence didn't convince us to change our minds. The words I had heard earlier echoed through my mind: Whose report will you believe, man's or God's? Yet, I had to be honest and tell her about the pain and not being able to stay on my feet for very long periods of time. She assured us it wasn't from anything she had done in the procedure.

The doctor referred me to three doctors. When we left the office I was in a daze and my head was spinning. When will it end? I was longing to get from under all these problems and get on with my life. To make matters worse, because of the exam I was in more pain. My husband and I prayed against all those bad reports that were spoken over me. I crawled in the back seat of the van to sleep, right after we prayed. There are times when we must rest in the Lord and lean not on our own understanding.

Proverbs 3:5 says, "Trust in the Lord with all your heart, and lean not on your own understanding. In all your ways acknowledge Him and He shall direct your paths."

The doctor told me to take it easy and stay off my feet. I wasn't sure how we'd get through this. Even while sleeping my mind drifted to piles of unwashed clothes. I knew I was too busy focusing on my circumstances, the dirty kitchen floor, and the wall-to-wall clutter, all of the stuff Mom organizes and puts away.

GOD WAS STILL IN CONTROL.

Nothing is too small or insignificant for Him. While all this was going on my mom had been ill. I felt unable to do very much for myself, and now my mother needed me also. I was unable to be there. Even if I did manage to fly there I'd be a hindrance rather than help. Those who are ill can hardly care for others.

When I dwelt on everything that was going wrong, I felt like I was losing my mind. How long will it take to climb this mountain and have these problems behind me? Where is my evidence of total healing? When will my "sentence" end? Yet, I had to close that negative door, looking toward God and my future.

Now I had to walk in faith, believing my life would get back to normal because God was healing me. God says that all things will work out to our good to those that love the Lord and put Him first. I was seeking after Him and putting my trust in the Master. God was in control now and even before I had the procedure done, I had to rest in the Master's lap, placing my entire life in His hands.

"Even youths grow tired and weary and young men stumble and fall; but those who hope in the Lord will renew their strength.

They will soar on wings like eagles; they will run and not grow weary, they will walk and not be faint." (Isaiah 40:30-31)

I was blessed with a husband who doesn't mind helping me with the cooking, laundry, and some of the cleaning. Life goes on and my life stayed pretty much the same. That's where the problem began. Here I was in the middle of my trial, longing for evidence of my miracle. When we get impatient with the journey we're on, it is time to stop and seek God for the answers.

It was easier to stand in faith the first week. As time went by my faith was getting smaller and smaller. What did I do? I needed a faith boost. The Bible states our faith grows by hearing the word of God. For me I needed to memorize a scripture that I could quote and rely on to give me the needed strength.

In reality it was so easy to look around at the situation and everything that I was unable to do. Looking at things this way, I started complaining. I wasn't being thankful in all circumstances, I wanted to be healed instantly and released from the pain I was in. Who could save me? I knew only God could. Yet, I cried out in despair rather than requesting help and seeking Him.

The dirty dishes piled high in the kitchen, the carpets really needed to be vacuumed, dirty laundry and clutter everywhere. In a weak moment I started feeling sorry for myself. I felt helpless to change my situation. I placed my hope on a shelf where it was accumulating dust.

No one would recommend going outside in a hailstorm, but that's exactly where I was, hanging on the side of the mountain in the pouring rain. Yet, not for long; God has allowed me to face these problems that I know I am helpless to solve on my own. I must turn to Him for the answers.

I wanted it all to end but not this way. Oh, please God, save me again! Crying out to God only knowing I needed to repent. I cried out, "Father, forgive me for turning my back on you and failing to be thankful in all circumstances." We are taking our eyes off Him and focusing on the problem. God hates it when we complain.

Proverbs 6:12-13 says, "A worthless person, a wicked man, Walks with a perverse mouth; He winks with his eyes, He shuffles his feet, He points with his fingers; He devises evil continually, He sows discord. Therefore his calamity shall come suddenly."

We don't start out being wicked, but every evil person I believe started down that road by complaining. It is with our mouths that we begin a gripe against God. To complain is really criticizing God for allowing bad things to happen to us. It tears down and never builds up. God is bigger than any circumstance we may be going through! What we are really trying to say is, "I don't like the things you are allowing to happen in my life." Yet, every bad experience should only draw me closer to God.

The next week, it was on to the hernia doctor. He said he couldn't tell but felt that, if I had a hernia, it is a very small one. It doesn't have to be operated on, just watched. Now, I also stood in faith to believe that the hernia was healed. I ask the nice doctor, "Can I go back to work now?" By this time my house had been neglected for over a month.

He smiled and said, "Oh sure, unless it causes you pain." I felt like saying I have been in pain watching the clutter grow higher like mounds of refuse. But instead I just shouted, "Yes! I can clean; I can't wait, look out dirt, I'm on my way," I replied. By now I have to explain to this doctor, who is looking at me as if I had lost my mind! "I just love to clean and with four children it's a good thing," I reply.

I wasn't healed instantly; it became a faith building process. God used this healing to help me grow. Day by day I claimed what I did not feel or see. I stood in faith that I was healed. I began by thanking God for healing me and stating how I felt in a positive way or not saying anything at all. Even my thoughts had to be monitored because negative thoughts will produce negative results. Well, there is such joy and excitement when God answers our prayers.

So much to regain it was actually a blessing to be able to cook and clean again. One part of my life seemed to be getting back to normal. Think how you would feel if you could no longer do one of your regular activities. Losing something is a real challenge. We hold on to the hope that it will be restored. We do our part, and ultimately, it is God who restores. All our **Hope** must be in the hands of the Restorer. Impossible **Hopes** are made possible through Jesus Christ. God is the God of impossibilities.

When I got back to the business of being a full-time mom, I soon realized that it was not over yet. If I stayed on my feet all day, or worked like I had in the past, the pain would return. I still couldn't do any lifting. I realized how much I'd taken my arms and muscles for granted. Our miracle is at hand as we close our eyes to what seems like reality and we open them to God's plan. I did know I was going through the healing process. As I waited for the adventure to continue, I knew there were still many mountains to climb.

Don't get me wrong; I had the procedure done for what I thought was a good reason. I had pain in my pelvic area for years. It came and went; yet we were never able to figure out the cause. I went to countless doctors.

In January, I did learn what was causing all the pain. All my organs in the lower abdomen were fused together from an earlier surgery twelve years ago. The scar tissue connected my uterus to the bladder on one side and the rectum or lower bowel on the other. Normally, the uterus floats in the abdomen.

We can really get ourselves in some predicaments. I listened to a doctor and hadn't sought God's will about having the procedure done. Now as the days seemed to drag slowly by, my health was getting better. God answered my prayers for healing even when I was the one who got myself into this mess.

The pain that had started out being a nuisance turned out to be the very thing for which I thanked God. Why? It is through adversity that we grow. I began to focus, not on the pain, but on the possibilities. They were limitless. God used the pain to allow me to see beyond my circumstances.

Now, in the middle of the situation, we have two choices: to give up or hang in there. It was a long journey and in the midst of it, I questioned how long it would take to get to the top of this mountain. By asking the question "Why me?" I was left to feel sorry for myself. But that didn't do anything positive to help. Would the pain ever end and my life gets back to normal? Never could I have imagined how unprepared I was to face the journey. Being victorious wasn't just a matter of getting healed. It was how I chose to live each day, in victory or defeat.

Living for God meant looking for praiseworthy things in my life, climbing the mountain of pain, knowing God was in control. I choose to be happy and seek just what I could learn from my circumstances. It was a long journey; one day it would be over. How I faced each day mattered more than how it would turn out. It is the steps in the process that change us. I learned just how much my family depended on me. I had to live being dependent on them, leaning more on God. It was the reverse of how things had been in my life. It was a humbling experience, one God used for my good.

You might think that the pain would be the same. In reality, if we focus on the negative it seems to worsen. Giving up doesn't remove us from the attack; it only gets worse. Rather than giving in, I ask, "What is God trying to teach me?" How will this experience enhance my life and help me to grow? God never meant that we would walk through the flames of the fire unchanged. The day came when I thanked God for the pain. Why? From it I became less independent and relied more on the Lord. Well the journey was long and I believe that God didn't send this problem my way. But He allowed it to be used for my good.

My prayer changed when all I wanted was to get closer to God. The circumstances showed me how to take one step closer, that's where I needed to begin. Thank you, God, for the pain you allowed me to endure. My life void of your voice would have brought far more pain than I could ever have imagined.

We know in this complex world, there is so much to learn. Yet, many times there are important things that we have forgotten. Growing closer to God required that I set aside a quiet time to listen. While praying, remember to take the time to have a two-way conversation with the Master. Want to get to know Him better? You must be willing to   **LISTEN.**

What is in store for me? Well, there is no need to worry about the future. From where I'm standing there is no way I can make it to the top, Lord, no way. In that solitary moment as I paused I heard a voice say, "You can make it. I'll be right here beside you. I will never leave you."

I took a deep breath and knew it was time to move on. Life brings so many difficult situations and problems with no formula answers. I get caught up in the situations and become so perplexed by the problems that without realizing it I am trying to figure everything out on my own. It amazes me how far I go before I realize I've left God behind.

I have been caught up in the business of getting things done. It is a dangerous thing, facing the storm alone. It gets worse when you're on a cliff. My life depends on God and it is when I'm alone that I begin to realize just how much. I need the forgiveness of Jesus and the empowering of the Holy Spirit, my life depends on all three.

Romans 8:24 states, "But if we must keep trusting God for something that hasn't happened yet, it teaches us to wait patiently and confidently." (The Living Bible) We are saved by trusting and trusting means looking forward to getting something we don't yet have. That's what **Faith** is: relying on God to give us what we need.

CHAPTER 7

THE LEDGE

It is very slippery and wet; as I look out into the distance, I notice it is growing darker. There is the sound of thunder and I begin to wonder. When will it begin to rain? A faint smell of the upcoming storm answers my question. I swing my backpack from my shoulders, lower it to the ground, and begin searching for my raingear. The rain begins fiercely beating against my body. The wind pushes me against the jagged edges of the rock protruding from the side of the mountain. I must find a safe place to weather out this storm.

Carefully looking down I peered over the edge at everything that was below. Suddenly, without warning my feet are leaving solid ground. I began slipping and sliding, out of control; my arms were flailing in a desperate attempt to save myself. I'm desperately grasping at rocks and gravel, trying to find something solid to hang onto. I was sure my life would end and with all the wind knocked out of me, I'd landed on what appeared to be a ledge protruding from the mountain. Straining to catch my breath, I realized just how close I came to dying. This ledge saved my life; rather God used it to rescue me. I'm stranded here but alive! When I fell over the edge, I knew the outlook didn't look good; off the side of a mountain is no place to fall.

What caused me to lose my footing? Oh, yes, now I remember, I was looking at my circumstances, caught up in the calamity of my life and everything that was going wrong! The winds of resistance begin to blow and the events of my life caught me off guard. Everything began swirling round and round until I was unable to distinguish which way to go. Life gets rough when we are in the middle of a storm. Just like Peter when he took his eyes off Jesus.

In Matthew 14:27-30 it states, "But immediately Jesus spoke to them, saying, "Be of good cheer! It is I; do not be afraid." And Peter answered Him and said, "Lord if it is You, command me to come to You on the water."

So He said, "Come." And when Peter had come down out of the boat, he walked on the water to go to Jesus. But when he saw that the wind was boisterous, he was afraid; and was beginning to sink..."

Don't we all do the same thing even today? God, if it's your will, we think. While we proceed to keep our eyes on God all will go well. But the minute we look around at what seems impossible to us (the circumstances), the boisterous winds cause us to fail. Hopeless describes our lives when we base our decisions on our fears. For that single moment in time we lose our faith in God. We forget that the master we serve is larger than any danger we might face. He is ready and able to rescue us.

When Peter was beginning to sink at the end of verse 30, "he cried out, saying "Lord save me!" I remember when my problems overwhelmed me. How do I solve all these problems? Emotionally I had to grow or I would be sinking just as Peter did. The mountains of problems that were impossible for me to solve became the miracles that we celebrated; it was a good day. I look at things too many times with human eyes; from our viewpoint it looks bad. But our God is still a God of miracles if we just keep our eyes on him. Peter took his eyes off Jesus.

What I would like to point out is that Jesus had not moved and He did save him. Peter started out hearing and seeing only the Master. He wasn't bothered when Jesus asked him to do the impossible. So he was able to walk on the water! What went wrong? We all know that he took his eyes off the source of his power.

"And immediately Jesus stretched out His hand and caught him, and said to him, "O you of little faith, why did you doubt?" as stated in Matthew 14:31. Romans 8:26, explains, "And in the same way-by our faith the Holy Spirit helps us with our daily problems and in our praying... We have to be plugged into the power source. Standing in faith we are many times asked to do things that don't seem to be in our best interest. Now, if I were in charge, I'd do this. We must remember to make the decision to yield to God's will in every situation.

At this particular time, I felt stranded, as one might feel perched high above the ground on a mountain ledge. I was unable to move, paralyzed with fear. The circumstances were life changing. My mom had been ill since Christmas. In April, she told me that she was going to have an operation in May. Even before that phone call I had been guided by the Holy Spirit to visit our relatives in Ohio the first week of May. Mom called today, telling me her surgery is scheduled for Monday, May 3. Everything was falling into place.

God reminded me not to change my plans about going to Ohio that week. I questioned in my mind, why the warning? That was before the wind of resistance started blowing. This was to be a trip the entire family would make. We have four children living at home. All of the children were adopted as older children.

They are Jonathan, Michael, Sarah, and Rebecca. Of these four, three of them have symptoms of attention deficit disorder, known as ADD. The two boys have symptoms of ADHD, attention deficit with hyperactivity. Any type of change in their routines causes hyperactivity.

Our youngest child, Betty Rebecca, was very reluctant to go to school those last few days. I told her that soon school would be out and we would be on our way to Ohio. Trying to motivate her, I had failed to think about the consequences. That was a big mistake that I didn't realize at the time!

Only days later the news had spread. Betty told her brothers and sisters. Well, when everyone knew from the oldest to the youngest, Michael was sent to verify it. "Betty says we are going to Ohio after the last day and school," stated Michael. "Yes, that's right," I said. Now the rumor had been confirmed.

The children were already full of energy because summer vacation was right around the corner. Now they had another reason to be excited. The two events happening simultaneously resulted in complete chaos. The children ran through the house. My husband and I fell exhausted into our bed every night.

Their behavior was so bad that at one point my husband asked me, "Would you rather fly to Ohio by yourself?" The thought had already occurred to me. Being realistic I had to ask myself, "Would it be safe to take these children on a 650-mile trip?" Under these circumstances it didn't look good. The storm was spinning round and round so fast I wasn't sure which way to go.

Had I really heard from God? I prayed about our dilemma and the words "divide and conquer" came to mind. Then I heard a voice say, It will be all right; the children will settle down the moment you leave for Ohio. With the end of the storm in sight, I went to tell my husband what the Lord had spoken to me. We should go as planned.

There was so much confusion in the midst of our storm. As the winds blew harder and harder, we struggled to stand firm.

Our greatest effort was put in not getting caught up in what was happening around us. God was guiding us to take our eyes off of the situation and keep them on Him. God could calm the winds at anytime.

From one moment to the next, we must depend on God to lead us. It means our plan is to follow His, even when His plan seems impossible. Our confirmation that it was His plan came when He turned the impossible around. The moment our van started backing out of the driveway, my husband and I looked at each other and smiled. Our children were all quietly sitting in their seats ready for the trip!

God must order my steps and, from one moment to the next, all I know is that I'm following Him. God reminds us that He is ultimately in control. Looking at the situation, if I had been in charge, I know I would have flown to Ohio, by myself. God was leading us and He said, "Go as planned," and we did. God knows our future and is making daily decisions on our behalf, knowing what lies ahead.

We all want to be in the driver's seat. The driver is the one steering the car. We must be the passengers allowing the Holy Spirit to lead us. Relinquish your steering wheel and let God set the course and destination for your life. Being led by the Holy Spirit is exciting because we never know where He'll lead us or what we will be asked to do next.

The rewards are never-ending when we allow ourselves to be Spirit led. There is such joy and satisfaction in serving God. We are laying down our lives, crucifying self, and living for God. Crucifying self is the first step as we begin living a Christ-filled life, allowing Christ to live in us and through us.

God can't accomplish His will without willing people. Christ gave everything. Now God is asking us take up His cross and follow Him. We can't really be His unless we are willing to do His will.

A servant submits to his boss's or master's authority. We can't be the master of our lives and serve the only true master, God. Going out on that ledge allowed me to keep the world at bay. I really just wanted to be left alone. While sitting there I found plenty of time for prayer and to fast.

CHAPTER 8

THE PIT OF DISOBEDIENCE

Disaster strikes and my mind begins spinning, turning, twisting out of control, going back in space and time, speeding faster and faster back. Flashing through my mind were the events of this past year from my mother's operation and convalescing. She only seemed to be getting worse. I tell myself this isn't really happening, it just has to be a nightmare as I relive over and over again the bad news. Lost in a nightmare I thought I was having, just as the morning sun dawned, so did my reality. I didn't want to talk to anyone. I just lay in bed in a daze, trying not to think. I awaken to the realization that my bad dream was in actuality my life! Why did my mother have to die?

Tears trickled down my cheek and I tried to block out everything I was feeling inside. I wasn't ready to let her go. Yet she had indeed passed away. Here I was just like a small child feeling left behind. Yes, it was truly a time to mourn. I lay in my bed watching scenes of my life go by.

I couldn't return to the past, I knew that, and now the future would be forever changed. I felt helpless to change the events that had begun unfolding months before. If only it had been just a nightmare, but this was in fact my life. My mother had died. We all have to face the loss of a loved one in our own way. The facts don't change and death is inevitable. I don't think I would have ever been ready for my mom's death no matter how long she lived.

Seeking a solitary refuge where everything around me was calm, peaceful, and secluded is what I felt I needed. I so longed to get away. How will I make it? Not on my own endeavors. I have learned that I do need others. Even though I know they won't always be there for me. There is only one way! I'm not really alone; it is God that I can depend on. The very hands that created me are holding me.

Hour and hours have gone by it was then that I decided to look for a way of escape. I noticed a rather large vine dangling over my head. Carefully hugging the mountainside with my left arm, I stretched out my right arm toward the vine. Could I reach it? I found my arms too short to reach what seems to be my only way. Maybe if I use a rock to boost myself up I'll be tall enough to reach the vine.

I knew it was risky, but it seemed to me that there was no other choice. So I grabbed onto the vine dangling above me and as I looked down the view of the vast pit below frightened me immeasurably. Everything below looked very scary to me. The ledge was such a safe temporary place to be right now. Yet, I couldn't survive there forever. But I also didn't want to leave this sanctuary for the unsure passage of a branch merely a swinging vine to save me.

In the spirit I grasped the vine, leaving behind the solitary place of refuge the ledge offered. I stretched as far as my arms could reach. Flashing through my head, "What if I don't ..." Even though

I'm physically weak, surely I can. "I can't do this," I yelled out loud, "I'm scared I'll die." Squeezing my eyes tightly closed and leaning forward, I tried again! "I won't do this!" Just then my feet began to slip on the gravel of the ledge and fear gripped me on a higher level than I had ever encountered before. Suddenly my hands started burning.

I came to the end of myself and just as quickly the end of the rope. Tragically there was nothing left to hold onto! I started free falling off the side of this 200 foot mountain. I cried out to God in desperation! My destination is unknown as I'm thinking about all the plans I hadn't accomplished yet. In the spirit I instantly knew why this had happened.

Why did my mom have to die?

Six months later.

And now my dad was gravely ill. My father was rushed to the hospital with a heart attack. The small local hospital transported him to Dayton, Ohio's heart hospital. After several days he was allowed to go home to wait for triple bypass surgery. I wanted to drive up so I could visit and spent time with him just in case the Lord decided his time was up.

When I spoke to him on the phone Dad tried to persuade me to wait until the snow was gone. The roads would be better then, he said. But I reassured him that Ray would check the Internet for hazardous conditions of the freeway and the predicted weather report before I left. So I made all the necessary arrangements for after-school care for our children and began packing.

I really wanted to take someone with me. I invited a friend; however, she couldn't make it. I felt in my spirit that someone was going with me. It is approximately a twelve-hour drive. I took along my best friend the Holy Spirit along with some music on several cassette tapes. The drive was a refreshing one because there was plenty of quiet-time to pray, listen, and sing. I stopped in Kentucky to go shopping and arrived at my brother Michael's house before dark. The next day I drove on to Greenville, Ohio to my dad's home.

It was snowy and cold. I called my sister Lisa and she came over to visit. We actually went out for a walk. We made plans to go the lawyer's office early the next day to sign the final paperwork for our mother's estate. She was upset and didn't want to go. Later on that day, Eleanor, my older sister, called. She said, "You and Lisa don't have to go to the lawyer's office." Eleanor had picked up the paperwork and had taken the legal document to Michael's house.

I'm ashamed of the next words that came out of my mouth. I said, "I won't call Lisa and tell her because she might change her mind about signing." Something rose up in my spirit and I knew I had sinned. I was more concerned about getting the money than my sister's feelings. It was cold and snowing the next day when I arrived at McDonald's. I circled the restaurant, parked the truck, and went inside to wait for Lisa.

She arrived and we decided to go in her car. I walked right by my truck. "Lisa," I said. "I better move my truck because we'll be gone a long time." On the way back to my vehicle I slipped on a patch of ice under the fresh morning snow. I heard my arm snap. As I was looking up, my sister got out of her car and asked, "Kay, are you all right?" No, I broke my damn arm," I replied.

If only it was a bad dream, yet, the nightmare keeps repeating itself. I remember being out of control and falling faster and faster toward the black hole of doom. I was going down and I blamed everyone else. Running from God I was out of control. When all of a sudden I relived that moment when I slipped and began falling into this ugly pit. I never meant to fall; I was sure I could stand up on my own.

Suddenly I'm awakened to the sounds of screaming, realizing they are my own and nothing had changed. When my true allegiance was self-seeking, it was as if I had walked off the side of the mountain. It nearly cost me my life. We become idolaters because we have stepped out of God's will. Self becomes number one while putting our desires above God's. I haven't gotten to the point where I've given in and let Him completely reign over every area of my life.

It is our Heavenly Father who loves us and will turn every disaster into something good eventually in our lives. God loves us that much. Relying on self, we lack everything. His knowledge and power is available to all those who put their trust in Him. When we stand on our own human strength there is always a price to pay. "I'm begging you, God, please forgive me for my greed and for questioning your will for my life. I need to feel your presence; I need you." The tears were streaming down my face and I was truly sorry for my many sins.

Please forgive me, God, for taking so much for granted. I wasn't willing to surrender it all. Rescue me from this place of self-sufficiency where my life revolves around me. I wanted to be in charge, imprisoned in a realm that no one seems to understand. I cling to reality trying to focus my attention, as I stare in a trance-like state; I'm hiding. The mountains in my life caused me to lose touch with reality. Everything that was dear to me was crushed, now I feel so empty, cold, and alone.

Then I began to place my trust in God, my hope in a future serving Him with a pure heart. My inner peace returned and as time went by, the ache in my heart was shrinking. I knew I couldn't change the past, but possibly the future. In God's presence is where I need to be. I began to pray for His divine deliverance first, thanking Him for my life. "I need you more than ever. Forgive me for putting my desires above yours, God." I knew that I needed to surrender and let God control my life. "Lord, you're all that I need."

God never left my side; He strengthened me and gave me a new hope for tomorrow. He picked me up and held me tightly and I knew I wouldn't have to stay in that awful pit of despair, lost forever. As I thanked the hand of God for everything, the tears were trickling down my face.

My children got to see Grandma one last time, because we listened and followed His plan. How guilty we would have felt if we hadn't. God's plan allowed for that last visit. He had also strengthened me that year. The problems that I faced helped me grow so close to God that I could make it even through my mother's death. I finally learned that life's goodness isn't based on circumstances but upon God's love for us that never changes. Racked with pain from the fall I found myself in a cheerful mood. Through it all, God will never abandon us. It is we who turn away.

Thinking what might have happened without Him, I sigh and tremble. Then I'm reminded of what I need to do, praise Him. "My hope is in you, Lord. Thank you for rescuing me." I began singing song after praise song to my God. "You're all that I need." Your presence is here. When I opened my eyes I was no longer in that desolate sinkhole. I found myself on the mountaintop overlooking the valley below.

God rescued me and set my feet on higher ground. I'm watching the beautiful sunrise and praising God for His forgiveness and awesome power. Every new day His mercies are brand new and miracles abound. He has painted me a masterpiece and in His presence is where I long to stay. "Where would I be right now if it weren't for you, God? Your presence is all that I need. Glory to God!"

CHAPTER 9

THE MOUNTAIN TOP

Every new day your presence is strong here in my heart at the break of dawn. On this beautiful mountaintop with the breathtaking view of the sun, a new day begins. I know the hands of God must have placed me here. Thank you for your healing touch and for giving me everything that I need. With every breath I take, I thank God. With all that I have, I worship my Lord, Redeemer, and friend. Wash over me cleaning me through my greatest love is you. Draw me nearer into this place where the spirit of my loving God hovers. It is you God that is awesome and full of grace. I just want to say thank you, God! Thank you!

There is such a sweet presence of the Lord as the new day dawns that I can't wait to spend time with Him. There is a praise song that reminds me of our loving God. The words of the song are, "I surrender to your love ...." I couldn't comprehend what it meant at first. I could understand it if we replaced the word "love" with "will." I surrender to your will, but the song didn't use that word. How are we supposed to surrender to God's LOVE?

The love of God surpasses our intelligence to even comprehend it. When we don't deserve it He loves and blesses us. God not only sent Jesus to die for our sins so He could erase them and declare us not guilty, He loads us down daily with more benefits than we could count: blessings from heaven, and today God has answered my prayer and removed the pain. I'm completely healed, jumping for joy.

The day has arrived and my trial is over. Standing on the mountaintop I was basking in His glory! With my new attitude life could only get better. I never could have climbed the mountains alone. God was right there guiding me all the way and teaching me. He kept me there until I got it right.

From this mountaintop, everything below looks so small. The difficulties seem trite. With the past behind me I was ready to live. Looking up, I notice an even larger MOUNTAIN in the distance. Is that where I'm going? That mountain looks awfully big. It's a giant among mountains.

I felt happy to be able to work again, although I missed all the help everyone had given me while I was ill. I was changed in a way that was so different from before. Prior to this illness on a regular day I rarely called on God. I was on the front lines alone; God was backing me up: He was my troubleshooter, and I wasn't facing Him.

We lacked a closeness that I knew God really longs for His children. God needs us. Now God goes before me, and I have learned that anything out of God's will is wrong. Our relationship was all one-sided. I did all the talking; praying was always begging God for what I wanted. Oh, I called on Him all right, but only when life got rough.

Here I am in this beautiful place; it could be any place as long as my eyes are set on you, God. The pain is gone! I just want to say, "Thank you for changing me and forgiving me for everything." I need to worship you. I just want to say, "Thank you for my life, my strength, for all that I am because of my Lord."

I have tried to keep my eyes focused on God and keep reminding myself that He is in control. Suddenly all the negative things like worry, anger, fear, grief, and all their byproducts like anxiety, negativity, strife, and doubt have no place in my life, because I was transformed during this rough period of my life.

Seekers seek the will of God for their lives. He disciplines us out of the abundance of His love. When we surrender to His love we recognize that He loves us so much and knows what is best for us. We are obedient and put His will above ours. A will or document left by a relative states what your inheritance will be, while your will leads you away from a personal relationship with God. God wants to bless us beyond anything we can even imagine. God will give and freely you salvation and forgiveness of your sins. What He longs to give you His will, if you seek Him. When you are out of God's will you will not reap all the benefits. A disobedient child is not given the request of his heart. Nor will you receive what you have longed for.

Timing is everything; the closer we get to God the tighter the rules. A small sin will slip you up. Sin starts small and works its way into your life, growing bigger and bigger. Buried under my sin was pride. I wanted my way and I was going to get it. That attitude always comes with a price and leads us away from the Father. Sometimes we are going the right way but at the wrong time. Listen closely for the voice of the Holy Spirit to lead you.

When a policeman states you are under arrest, we should say I surrender. We all know why: He has authority; if we don't obey we will get hurt. It is because we need to obey authority. God is over us and we need to surrender everything to Him.

Many times in life I was blessed because God didn't answer my prayers and give me what I asked for. God knows everything and blesses me with an abundance of everything that I need. My life is a blessing from God. What I make of it will be a blessing to others and myself if I allow God to show me how.

Give me a fresh anointing for this journey. I need to pray with a right attitude for His kingdom's business. My life touches many lives and now, as I have been given a new assignment; it is easy to feel overwhelmed. There is so much to do; how will I find the time?

"Thank you, God, for allowing me to be tested." God will use everything we go through for our good if we will seek Him first. Help change me from the inside out so I can truly love others; love them like Jesus loves me. I asked God to let me start over again loving, living, and surrendering everything to His will.

Where are you today? Are you on the mountaintop where everything is going well? Or have you fallen in the pit of despair, lower than you've ever been? Don't give up hope. When you have bottomed out, there is only one way to go and that's up. Or are you on the ledge of learning to depend on God? I am here to tell you never give up but allow God to rescue you no matter where you are. God is the answer to every situation or season you are in.

CHAPTER 10

OUR MISSON

The more you are doing for God, the more battles you'll experience. Many times the devil will fight against you all the way. He doesn't want God's will to be done in your life. God will empower you with every weapon to defeat your enemy. The devil hates successful people living for God. Even as a Christian, I am most miserable when I reflect self in place of God. A mirror reflects our outer image, but God knows the motives of our hearts. God will equip us with everything we need; yet He still wants us to do the legwork. It starts by falling on our knees in prayer, seeking to find God's will and dream for our lives.

"Every step I take, I take with him," are the words of a song. God's plan is a highway that brings us closer to our destination. It will require all the love you have to give and more. Beyond self is a storehouse of God's strength. Dreams don't just happen; they take planning and hard work.

My "DREAM" started when our last child left home to go out on his own. I was saddened by the emptiness of our home. In my heart, I grieved the loss of my children. They were all grown. Everyone told me to just get over it and enjoy what could be the best time in my life, only the feelings intensified as I tried to move forward with my life.

Meanwhile, my husband didn't share my burden. He was happy with our just-two status and definitely didn't want any more children! Later I asked God to take this feeling from me or zap my husband with it. Gradually God changed him, birthing a mission for children in his heart as well.

There were times when I cried out to God to fill the empty space in my heart. "Please, give me a child to love." My feelings were so intense that I had a recurring dream of a baby crying outside my door. Years later, I realized that I could have actually heard my children crying on the very day they were born and I wrote this poem:

> On the day you were born
> I heard you cry.
> I search everywhere for you.
>
> On the day you were born,
> I heard you cry.
> And it brought tears to my eyes.
> I looked everywhere for you.
> But you couldn't be found.
>
> On the day you were born.
> I longed for a child
> To hold in my arms
> To fill the empty space,
>   in my heart.
>
> On the day you were born.
> I waited for you.

I didn't know then,
What I do know now.
That you were waiting too.
For a mother to love you like I do.

We pondered maybe foster care would be the answer. No, that would be too difficult for us. We would just get attached and then have to give the child back, or so we imagined. That seemed more than either and us could bear. Adoption was an idea. I had only one fear: that we would be turned down. That certainly was showing my lack of faith. God's will never fails unless you give up. If you decide to let God down, He'll search until He finds another willing person ready and available to do what He wanted you to do. If God has planted something in your spirit you need to be willing so God's dream for your life can begin.

We received the mound of paperwork and started the process. Soon we were enrolled in parenting classes. I moved 160 miles away, to take my first teaching position. This did lengthen the entire process. The waiting seemed endless. Last on our list was to have a home study done and wait for the right child. We did wait and wait three long years.

All this time my heart ached. I wondered, "When, God, when? At the end of my second year of teaching I told my husband I was giving up. He got so excited, saying, "Now God will answer our prayers because we've done everything possible, except turn it over to Him." I thought my husband was crazy, but I also prayed he was right.

At the beginning of summer we received the call we had long awaited. We were asked if we'd like to adopt a nine-year-old boy. If we decided to adopt this boy, we may never be able to adopt more children. As much as I wanted a child I was hesitant because we had wanted a sibling group. If we could only adopt one child,

I wanted it to be a girl. But I did pray and seek God's will for our lives.

God told me this boy needed unconditional love, and that we needed him also. Would I follow my plan or God's? Later, there would be times when I'd think, "Why did we think we could do this?" Then I remembered God's words. This was His will and He would show us how. We had wanted children, just not such a difficult one. Our dream took hard work. It was by far the hardest emotional experience we'd gone though. Today, he is a blessing to have and the answer to our prayers. God was faithful to answer our prayers as we remained committed to Him.

God had selected us to be Jonathan's parents. Yet, we had wanted more than one child. That was still our dream two years later. Jonathan didn't want to be an only child, either. He had been praying for brothers and sisters. Jonathan had definitely made more progress than had been predicted.

We decided to ask the agency if we could adopt more children. They agreed partly because of Jonathan's excellent progress. We began the long process of getting all the paperwork ready and had prepared ourselves for the long wait. We had waited three very long years before Jonathan was placed in our home. While at work about a month later, I received a phone call.

The caseworker wanted to know if we would be interested in adopting three more children. The first question I asked was whether they were boys or girls. After she informed me that the oldest was a boy and he had two sisters, I told her I couldn't answer for my husband but that I was definitely interested. I was so excited I couldn't wait to share the news with Ray.

Meanwhile every evening we prayed, if this was truly God's will for us, bring these children to our home. I had already committed our lives to God's will praying for the three of us and the three children we had yet to meet. Two more months went by and we heard nothing. I knew that they were just asking if we were interested. There was no commitment on their part. They probably found another family to adopt the children, I thought. I had some paperwork that needed to be turned in to the agency. Rather than mail it I decided to deliver it in person.

Our caseworker thanked me for dropping off the papers. I stood there, uncomfortable for a moment, wondering what to say. She excused herself from the room, stating she was looking for a co-worker. She returned and introduced me to our new caseworker. She stated that he would be the caseworker for the children. She asked him if he had a picture of the three of them to show me.

We talked and made plans for everyone to meet. It was then that I knew we were to be blessed again. On December 17, 1999, the children came to live with us until they became legally adopted. It was the best Christmas present my husband and I had ever received. God blessed us far beyond our dreams; now we had two boys and two girls.

Our vision began with a deep longing in my heart that wouldn't go away. God changed my husband's heart, moved us "180" miles so that we could adopt these four special children. We were open to what God had for us. Our first son was supposed to be the only child we could adopt. We knew that it was God's will. Stepping out in trust brought us full circle back to our desire. God blessed us with more than we ever dreamed of because we surrendered to His will.

God's plan is by far superior to any we could imagine. It starts by surrendering to His will. We need to be totally dependent on God. He will never try and force us to follow Him. We make that choice every day. It is a good thing! It is something we should do every day. Seeking to get closer to God allowed me to see when I turned and went the opposite direction. Pleasing God wasn't my heart's desire.

Psalms 40:8 states, " I desire to do your will, O my God; your law is within my heart!"(NIV) Delight begins the moment I step out and force myself to do something that I know God is asking me to do. Many times it is something I'd never do unless God asked me to. My first step in drawing near to God is to seek Him daily. All I want is to hear is His voice and follow Him. The Holy Spirit is my guide and helper. When we were first saved, it is easy to fall back to our old way of doing things. The new birth brings about many changes. We are given a brand new start, just like our adopted children.

God adopts us and we become His. Our adopted children were Michael 9, Sarah, 8, and Rebecca, 4. They were supposed to come to our home four times for weekend visits prior to coming to live with us. On the second weekend, we decided that we'd skip getting them that third time. It was too heart-wrenching sending the children back to their foster mother.

Rebecca would start crying at the mention of returning. She would jump into my arms, putting a death grip around my neck. She would hang on, wrapping her legs around me, as if her life depended on it. We just didn't have the heart to pry her loose, screaming one more time. To her it was as if her life was being ripped away from her and she had to return to the old way. It was fear that gripped her. She had bonded already and believed we were her forever family.

She was afraid of losing the love she had never experienced before. Her fears were very real! She was definitely afraid of losing her new life. She didn't want to go back even if it was only temporary.

When we come to God, He totally loves and accepts us just the way we are. Making the decision to accept Jesus is the most important choice of our lives. We are adopted by God just as we are. We should be like Rebecca, never wanting to return to our presaved days. People will not be able to pry us loose. Our old lifestyle will be a thing of the past if we cling desperately to God.

We are sold out for Jesus, with a brand-new life! We hold on to that new life knowing it offers us more than our past existence. Rebecca was no different. She longed to hold onto the family that offered her love, acceptance, and hope for the future.

Seekers seek to do God's will and it begins the moment you realize who you are. You are a child of God who has died to self-will and now live for God eagerly ready to serve Him. We become brand-new born again to live for Christ. When we seek and serve God our lives are blessed more than we could ever imagine.

The blessings begin as we seek God's will for our lives. If only we could be like Rebecca, fighting fiercely about going back, holding on to our new life in Christ at all costs. Always remember that successful people fall down, but they get right back up to try again. It's a brand-new day with endless possibilities and my journey continues. At the edge of the meadow lies a dense forest. I know that it isn't logical to go that way but God is calling me. I'll search for Him and seek Him daily. Then God will reveal His purpose for my life. I walk towards my destiny and the adventure that lies ahead.

CHAPTER 11

LOVING THE LOST

It is love that transforms us, the love of God, Christ, and the Holy Spirit. When I read Philippians 2:3, "Let nothing be done through selfish ambition or conceit, but in lowliness of mind let each esteem others better than himself," it reaffirmed what I'd been thinking. My actions didn't line up with the word of God. Change began when I meditated on being like-minded with Christ. We need to do everything with the same motive of Jesus: love.

Something to love and that needed my love brought with it more pain because I didn't know locked deep inside my heart was a hole that also needed to be mended. To freely love others as Jesus intended me to. I had to discover how much God loved me. Loving others unconditionally was impossible to do until I found myself at the foot of the cross looking up into the eyes of Jesus.

LOVE HAS THE POWER TO CHANGE ALL OF US!

Everything that I believed in went against the sin I allowed to creep into my life. I was ashamed of my actions and was desperate to change. How will I find the right path that will lead me safely through these woods? When we think God is not there, we realize we have truly lost our way; lost and all I can think about is all the people who have disappeared, never to be found.

I look in every direction only to find no clues as to which way to go. Many hikers will tell you they try to get their directions by finding the sun. Lost from God? Look for His Son to find your way. Jesus will assist you in finding a way to free yourself from the sin you're involved in.

I was honestly ready to get professional help, when I felt the Holy Spirit nudge me to take a class offered by our church. Seeking the need for direction in my life, I prayed that this class would change my life in ways that everything else I tried had not. I knew the moment I opened the book, that I could change with God's help. The transformation in me turned my failure around and it became my success.

Set free, I live in liberty. Others no longer threaten me when they lash out at me in anger; God's peace remains. I'm thinking, God, I know you're going to help me get through this, without turning on them like a mad dog! I don't want to say anything that will feel good at the time but that I'll regret later. To make matters worse I will have to ask them to forgive me whether or not they feel compelled to apologize. Also I want my actions to show God's love.

I hate when I mess up and treat the other person the way they are treating me. Hate can be very contagious, like a fast-growing disease. Yet, we have already been given the antidote and will not receive the disease, if we crucify the flesh and act out of the love we have received from Jesus.

The pressures of this life are too heavy to bear without Jesus standing up from within us. I can't figure out all the answers to my problems. But, I'm smart enough to seek the One who does. I'm crucified, born again, bought by the blood of Jesus. I am a child of God. Yet, victorious is what I can be with Jesus Christ who strengthens me. I've learned how to die to self and live for Him.

One incident that I recall was with my daughter Sarah, who was placed in our home for adoption. Locked inside of her were so much anger and hate. I had been unable to reach her or form any kind of relationship. I seemed to be her archenemy. One day she yelled at me, using bad language as well. What I did was run over to her and threw my arms around her. She was very uncomfortable. I spoke softly, "Sarah, I love you and I don't like it when you talk like that." She stood there stiff as a board, in shock I think. I hadn't given her anything to argue with.

We took one step closer because I showed her the mercy of God. Our natural response is to yell when someone screams at us. Try speaking very softly the next time you are in that situation and watch for their response. When was the last time God yelled at you? Our behavior should mimic His. I had tried everything that I knew to get through to her. She thought I was out to get her. I had to show her His love to win her's.

Jesus loved her even when she acted ugly. He knew the suffering she'd been through. The hate and anger she pushed deep inside had to come out. She had never been treated in a loving manner. She really didn't know how to love; even worse she didn't think anyone could love her.

Today she is my daughter and friend. It was that love that finally turned her around. Flesh had to die because in the flesh I wanted to slap her. But Jesus wanted me to show her love. Only God can equip us with what we need and help us navigate through difficult situations. God not only gives us what we need, He gives us His undying love, allowing us to love the unlovable. When someone has been nothing but mean to you, it is impossible in your own strength to show him or her kindness.

When love is given with nothing expected in return, it is unconditional love. Nothing melts the hearts of others more. God wants our help to win the lost. We don't have to feel love for the individual but be open to allow God's love to flow through us to them. I believe that the closer your relationship is to God the easier it is for you to get along with those difficult people, and eventually you will grow to love them.

Only God can equip us with what we need in difficult situations. God not only gives us what we need, He gives us the grace to walk in His love. People can be mean, and cruel, and it is impossible in our own strength to show them kindness. I am a child of God. Yet, victorious is what I'll be since I've learned how to die to self and live for Christ. Now, I'm making a positive difference in the lives of others.

Rising up on the inside of you will be the love God has for that person. He doesn't love the way they treated you, but He still loves them despite their sin. They are probably not even searching for God. The only chance they may have of finding Him is seeing Jesus in you. By loving those who seem undeserving, we show God's love to the world. We are God's ambassadors throughout the world.

In the Holy Spirit realm these dense woods are a lonely place to be in this season of my life when I'm searching. Which way should I go and how do I get there? Lord, lead me on this journey to follow your footprints. As I began searching through the brush, the thought occurred to me. How do I get there? By placing my trust in Him, listening for His voice to lead me. In the Holy Spirit realm, I breathe a sigh of relief. I've navigated through these woods before; up ahead I see what appears to be a wall. It is there that my destination awaits me.

CHAPTER 12

YOUR DESTINY

The decisions you make while seeking God's will for your life will take you on one of the greatest adventures of a lifetime. It begins the moment you surrender daily being led by the Holy Spirit. God has all the maps that plot out our lives. He knows the paths He wants us to follow. Do you have a dream or a vision that seems impossible for human hands? My husband Ray says, "That when he arrives in heaven the words he wants to hear are, "Well done my faithful servant. You have accomplished everything that I intended for you to do."

What would you do if you knew you couldn't fail? God may bless you with a million dollar idea. The million dollars won't just float down from heaven and land in your front yard. It will require great effort on your behalf. What God asks you to do won't always be convenient or enjoyable. There are days when I don't feel like working on the currant book I'm writing. Stating that, I must add the enjoyment that journaling brought me. It was such a release of negative energy and it helped me reflect back on how I'd grown closer in my Christian walk.

Success is promised as our reward. Reading God's word and following His plan will help us avoid a disaster. So follow God, by allowing Him to lead you. There is never a good reason for disobeying God. It didn't seem like disobedience at the time. Yesterday, I was busy cooking and making gingerbread houses. At the end of the day I thought, how much time did I give God today? Did the children receive all the attention they needed? Were the houses more important than all the things I failed to do?

I remember praying God: "Where are you? I can't feel your presence." I can't remember the last time the Holy Spirit touched me. I feel so utterly alone. I can't go on another day like this, I cried out to Him. I felt dry and brittle inside as if I'd gone months without water. Lost? Everything was so dry and I felt as if all the life was literally sucked right out of me. I was depressed and had many questions. How do I find my way back? Did I need to rededicate my life to God or was this only a dry period in my life?

Fasting and prayer came to my mind. I began thinking up excuses. Was I ready to do what I felt was required of me? Holy Spirit I need you, you're the only one that can help me run back into the loving arms of God. Reluctantly I said okay, but I had never successfully fasted and prayed before. I don't know how to do what you're asking, I told God. With man many things will seem impossible and will be impossible without God's help.

In the past when I had fasted I went without eating and said a few prayers during that time. Never had I set aside the time to pray continuously while fasting. God, I have never done this right before; but with your help I will. There was a desperation and feeling that I had to get back what was lost or missing from my life. I had no other plan in mind. Of course my next question was, how long am I fasting? One day? Okay, tomorrow is the day I've set aside.

Well, the next morning determination greeted me with the sunshine. I started praying early; by 9:00 I had an answer. God had called me to write and months earlier I had quit writing. There is only one way back to the Father if you have stepped out of His will. First acknowledge your sin and repent. Fasting and praying allowed me to redirect my life back to God. His plan is the only one I want to follow. We feel so utterly alone, trying to do the impossible; with God's backing the impossible becomes possible. Now I know God needs to be our number one priority. (Our Father who art in heaven, Thy Kingdom come, thy will be done.) God's agenda has to come first. Seek God first then His agenda is all we need to remember. All the other things we do are important to Him. But His will must be a priority and we cannot deviate from His plan

I don't profess to know what God has in store for you. Yet, I believe, in this season of your life you need to ask yourself this question. "How can I make a masterpiece of today?" Those are the words spoken by the late Billy Godwin. In your life right now, do you realize who ultimately should receive the glory for everything that you accomplish? My life is not my own but belongs to Jesus. I must crucify what I desire to do and surrender daily for His will to be done in my life.

Paul writes in Ephesians 3:20, "Now to Him who is able to do immeasurably more than all we ask or imagine, according to His power that is at work within us, to Him be the Glory in the church and in Christ Jesus through-out all generations, forever and ever! Amen.

The way you think determines your personality, character, and ultimately your destiny." states Terry Tripp from his book Unlocking God's Formula for Successful Living. When we obey we are His first choice. God will require you to do will be many things that you won't feel qualified or equipped to do. It is only through His power working in us activating our FAITH in Him that we are able to accomplish much. Proverbs 23:7 states, "As a man thinks in his heart so is he." **GOD'S** plan is the only one I want to follow. His plan for our lives is as unique we are. He is in control and needs willing people who will surrender 100% to Him. God created you for many specific needs He has on this earth. God has a plan for our lives that is greater than anything we could ever imagine. Our Lord has many great things in store for us. On this journey of discovery we will begin.

God knows the lessons we need to learn and many times He has to get us ready for the next assignment. Recently, I learned that our understanding of how God changes us is still flawed. God uses difficult situations and the trials we allow ourselves to get into to change our hearts, minds, and attitudes. In Pastor Chip Judd's sermon I learned that on the road to Damascus God changed Paul's direction, but it took a lifetime to transform Paul.

I believe that we have the tendency to remember the climactic, exciting events forgetting about the lifelong processes we must go through. God loves you just the way you are; but also loves you too much to leave you that way. I began searching through the bushes of the dense woods again. Which way should I go and how do I get there? I'm listening for His voice to lead me and by placing my trust in Him I wait. **I knew I needed to be led by the Father so I could get my directions from God.**

He won't keep you in the dark nor reveal His entire plan to you. God had to let me know the vocation; because I would never have discovered it on my own. It isn't something we can decide because God already has the plan. We have many things we're called to do. The journey of two people is never identical. Just like the forest, there are many ways to navigate through them to your destiny.

God holds the map for your life. Place your hand in His and you won't get lost.

I didn't like being lost either. The dark dense woods are a lonely place to be. How did I find my way? I had to be led by the Father so I could discover what I was called to do. My gifting wasn't what I would have thought. Choose to be lost or receive your directions from God. Yet what still amazes me is that God chose me to be a writer because I'm a terrible speller. I actually hated writing when I first began. Although I have to say that I did enjoy journal writing. I believe this is a biblical principal. Seek ye first the Kingdom of heaven and all these things will be added unto you.

I write because God called me to. Seeking to please Him writing became my heart's desire. So you to could actually hate something, but grow to love the very thing God created you for. I rely entirely on the Holy Spirit to give me the words to put on paper. It is only through His help that I can accomplish great things. **God uses ordinary people to do extraordinary things; so that we can give Him the glory**

I am called to be an evangelist as well. I have gone to foreign countries on mission trips. Everywhere all around you there's a mission waiting for your touch, an assignment with your name on it. Get busy where you are doing something positive for God and He will promote you. He will show you His plan. God opens the doors that no one can and He also promotes those who live to love pleasing God more than anything else. Christians should be constantly looking for ways to share the gospel.

You have already begun your journey and I pray you will continue to follow your destiny. No matter what you do if you realize that you are working for God you will be a success. God's plan for your life is a unique as you are. He has a custom-built plan for us and we were created for specific assignments on this earth.

In each season of your life there is an assignment with your name on it. God has a plan that is greater than any fantasy we could ever imagine.

God created you for a purpose. You are called to do many great things for our Lord. I don't confess to know all that God has planned for you. My prayer is that He will lead you as you follow that journey. As clues I've heard that what you'd love to be doing if money were no object might shed some light on discovering God's plan for your life.

However we must be willing to change. Carl Morris in one of his sermons talked about going into the Promised Land. It isn't the dread of the giants we face as much as it is the fear of the giants we must become and that is impossible unless you have a willing spirit. Where will you be in one year if you make no changes in your life not allowing God to change you? When we walk away from our heavenly Father and our personal relationship with him it is a dangerous place. We are no longer going to reap the benefits of being a kingdom child. We are on our own. We can't rely on our emotions and feelings. My life reflected a need that couldn't be met until I returned to God.

We are born to serve. Caught up in the business of raising children and running a home, I put God's business on hold. Actually I was disobeying God and putting priority on other things. I probably rationalized that I'd get back to His business later on. I was sure God understood, my family was very important. There didn't seem to be enough time to write. There were endless solutions once I made the choice to write.

Since I am a morning person I decided to write from 8 a.m. to 10 a.m. Last week I followed this plan. I am amazed, because the house never looked cleaner. Making God's will take priority I found I am able to do more in less time. My success is based on my obedience to God. The Bible states, in Matthew 7:7, "Ask, and it will be given to you; seek first the kingdom of God and you will find; and to him who knocks it will be opened."

When I look at my schedule it seems that there aren't enough hours in a day. What I failed to realize is God made time, the hours, and the days so I asked for Him to show me the solution. Sometimes we overlook the obvious. God is a God of miracles. I pondered how I was going to get everything done. I never had enough time doing things my way. We must seek to find our answer not in human hands but in our loving Father's.

I went to get our dirty laundry, but the hamper was almost empty. In my mind I couldn't figure it out. Yet, I do realize that our God is the same one that kept the Israelites' clothes from falling apart for the forty year journey. Surely He can keep ours clean. I was accomplishing more in less time. God was miraculously keeping things clean and with four children and a dog it was not short of a miracle. Even our home looked cleaner than when I was totally dedicated to it. When God gets involved everything that needs to be accomplished will be.

I have a poster of the Ten Commandments rewritten and named the "Ultimate Top Ten." The first commandment is: Nothing comes before God. Psalm 19 tells us the benefits of following God's laws. Verse 7 says, "The law of the Lord is perfect, converting the soul; The testimony of the Lord is sure, making wise the simple; The statutes of the Lord are right, rejoicing the heart; the commandments of the LORD is pure, enlightening the eyes; The fear of the Lord is pure. Enduring forever; The judgments of the LORD are true and righteous altogether. More to be desired are they than gold."... I'm now living my dream of becoming a Christian author. I know that I'm called to be a writer. I didn't always know that. My vocation isn't what I would have chosen for myself. When God is delegating what we should do, everything that needs to be accomplished will be. I always wanted to be in charge, never realizing how much

I limited what God could accomplish by allowing Him to be in control. Being led by the Spirit is one of the greatest experiences of my life. Today and everyday I still face the battle of His will versus mine.

Sir Winston Churchill stated, "There comes a special moment in everyone of our lives a moment for which we a uniquely qualified. In that moment he finds greatness and it is his finest hour." There should be many moments in our lives. We don't realize just how many people we influence by our words and actions. If the joy of the Lord is our strength even in time of adversity; then they will want what we have.

CHAPTER 13

POSITIVE OR NEGATIVE

Attitude determines our altitude. There is a Master and a master plan. In our life we will go through some rough times. "Yet our tongue can determine our atmosphere and destiny," writes Terry Tripp in his book *Unlocking God's Formula for Success.*

Be positive; an over comer is not a complainer. There is one quick way to get us lost and off course, taking us the wrong way every time, and that's by complaining. The Bible states in Philippians 2:14, "Do everything without complaining or arguing." (NIV)

Have you ever noticed that negative words make everything seem much worse? It isn't just words simply coming out of our mouths; it is the condition of our hearts and attitudes. The devil loves to hear us complain; to him it is like getting an A on his performance report card. We are questioning the Master and His plan for our lives.

The moment our attention is on our circumstances, we take our eyes off God. It is so easy to look around at everything that is going wrong. The winds of resistance seem to be trying to hold us back. We must remember to keep our focus on who's ultimately in charge. Thanking God for all of the blessings in our lives the good and what we view as bad.

We must be able to distinguish the resistance, its source, and if we did anything to cause it. Many times it is our stinking thinking that leads to complaining; idle words will alter our surroundings. On my journey through the forest I came to a clearing. There were two huge boulders set about six feet apart. On both sides of the rocks, the foliage was so thick I decided to go between them. I tried moving forward only it was impossible to get through. As crazy as it sounds it seemed like an invisible wall was holding me back.

"What is this, God?" What am I encountering? Pointing straight ahead I yelled, "That is the direction I want to go!" I stood dazed by my lack of progress. Leaning on what seemed like an invisible barrier, I yelled again, "Where are you now, when I need you?" Had God abandoned me?

When the resisting forces and our abilities fail we justify that this must not have been God's will, when we actually lost the source of our power. God never promised it would be easy. When the task at hand is more difficult than anything we've every accomplished, then we should realize we must rely on God. Yet, in the midst of the battle, I questioned His favor.

This experience of trying to get closer to God had gone haywire. I stated, "I give up; I can't go on any longer." Suddenly, with no warning, the wall that had held me back was gone. I lost my footing and was sliding down the ravine; just then I heard a waterfall. As I panicked, fear gripped me! I knew somehow what was the inevitable. I was sliding straight for the waterfalls!

It was then that I realized what held me back had been my guardian angel trying to protect me. My NEGATIVE words had released her. Words, just words, my words released her. No, they were not just words; much more than that, powerful words. I found

74

myself in dire straits. Doomed to a fate I'd never choose. But indeed I had.

When we start to complain about our circumstances, think about this. We could have missed hearing from God and have made a wrong choice. Our lamenting attitude makes us begin to question God and His ability to lead us. Things may not be going the way we want them to. Yet, God is allowing this problem in our lives as a learning experience. God is still in control. The very words we speak can be used to make things better or worse.

I never fully understood exactly why until I heard this message from Pastor Carl Morris. He quoted Luke 12:8, Where Jesus was speaking to thousands of people who had gathered around Him. "I tell you, whoever acknowledges me before men, the Son of Man will also acknowledge him before the angels of God." The words we speak either agree or disagree with the Bible.

If we agree with or have our words line up with what the Bible states, then our guardian angels that are sent to protect us will remain on the job. Pastor Carl Morris said "Yet, negative words bind our angels and render them ineffective to deliver us." If that wasn't bad enough, it gets worse. Demons are released by our complaining. "Only positive words can release the power of God."

God is still in control even if when I have taken our eyes off Him by concentrating on the negative. Disaster awaits me as I tumble down the steep incline headed for the waterfalls! Things are not be going well. Yet, God will allow bad circumstances into my life; Consider Job. The very words we speak can be used to save us or destroy us. My negative words had placed me on a pathway leading to my destruction. By complaining and resisting God, I ran right into the devil's camp. Even worse was my blindness of surrendering to the enemy.

Whom do we want working on our behalf? Telling everyone our mess only puts us on the devil's payroll. He may not be responsible for the mess we're in, but he loves it when we complain. We are stroking the devil's ego. None of us willingly want to give the enemy a compliment.

When we complain we resist God and run into the arms of Satan. Unknowingly we are surrendering to the enemy in defeat. Our guardian angels are bound and unable to come to our aid; demons are released to hinder us. Well, I am here to say that God is bigger than any problem I have, and I'm not going to worry and fret. He has the power and I have the faith to claim my victory because that's the kind of God I serve!

"I'm sorry God for my attitude, not allowing you to lead me and for all my complaining. I need you now more than words can express. Please forgive me, rescue me and take me in your arms. This isn't the direction I should have gone. Please don't let my sin of negativity lead to my doom. God, you alone are my safe sanctuary." God loves His children and blesses them. He blesses the saved and unsaved but how much more does he bless us? I believe we are receiving more than we ever could thank God for.

Inches from the edge of the falls I suddenly stop and crawl over to a safer place where I can rest. The view below reminds me of how close I came to going over the edge into the water below. That was so close; I must rest and thank God for rescuing me. Will your focus be on God and His goodness or on everything that is going wrong? It makes a big difference what we set our eyes on. Here is a good example of how different people viewed the same situation.

My husband and I had planned a romantic get away over the Easter holidays. We were waiting the vacation of a lifetime. We were counting down the days until our departure. Finally the day arrived and we were on our way. We drove from South Carolina, spent the night in a motel, and arrived in Miami on Sunday, in plenty of time to board the ship. We were excited and ready to begin our fantastic vacation.

That afternoon we were all on deck waiting for the mandatory lifeboat drill. We waited and waited and wondered why the delay. I thought they were just unorganized. After forty minutes, they announced over the intercom that the Coast Guard had found a problem with the ship's sprinkler system. It had to be fixed before we could set sail. They informed us that the problem could be dealt with and we'd set sail soon. Our forty-minute delay stretched to four hours.

The next day they informed us that the necessary parts had to be flown in from Europe. They were going to give every passenger on board a $400.00 credit to use on the ship. Because our seven day cruise would be shortened to 5 days at sea. Each day brought more and more delays. Until finally it was announced that sailing would be impossible. Apparently the necessary repairs would not be done in time for the ship to sail.

To be perfectly honest; I did spend a few minutes feeling cheated out of our romantic vacation to exotic places. I come from a long line of complainers. So looking at things positively is a challenge. When we are out in the world, it is so easy to look at everything from the devil's point of view. Pessimists state, if it weren't for bad luck I'd have no luck at all.

My husband was quick to remind me that this vacation was practically free. They were going to refund our money and pay for another cruise at a later date. The cruise lines allowed us to stay on board, eating and enjoying the entertainment. During the day they provided bus excursions into town, the beach, shopping, or sightseeing. The cruise line even paid our way into all the attractions.

We rested and had a very good time, unlike those who chose to complain for the entire week. We chose to be thankful for our vacation. We were not bored and on Thursday, we headed for Jacksonville, Florida, to visit two of our sons Justin and Joshua.

Many people on the ship were bummed out about the circumstances. I knew God was in control. If He didn't want us to set sail, then I didn't want to go either. I told several people that I believe in the divine will of God; He may have intervened on our behalf.

What really mattered wasn't why we didn't sail. But rather how we would respond to this test. How miserable we would have been if we had sat around complaining and focusing on the negatives. Our vacation was like no other; what an adventure! We really enjoyed ourselves! God, our source of happiness, never left us, because He dwells in the presence of those who praise and thank Him. With the money they refunded we were able to take our family on a cruise. The next summer, Ray and I took our original free cruise compliments of NCL. So in actuality we received three really great vacations for the price of one.

I also remember the time that I focused on everything that was going wrong. The Bible clearly tells us in Philippians 2:14, "Do all things without complaining." Have you ever noticed that growing weary starts with a negative attitude? I remember stating, "I can't do this, it's just too hard."

I had lost my cool and yelled at my children. Seeking to cool down, I paced back and forth outside our home. I cried out in frustration, "God, I can't do this!" His reply was, "You don't have to, just allow me to work through you." For the first time when trouble seemed to fall all around me I felt secure knowing I was not alone. In my strength it was impossible. God wanted to use me and I felt honored again.

Don't we do the same thing today? God, we cry out, if it is you and your will for our life then all goes well as long as we keep our eyes on Him. Yet, the moment we take our eyes off of God we fail.

It is so easy to look around at everything that is going against us. The winds of resistance that are trying to hold us back. But we must be able to stand and distinguish the resistance and more important is it's source.

Your journey depends on keeping your focus on God's will and your attitude positive. Your path is the one that's right for your life. The journey will be the greatest adventure. In your life there will be mountains to climb, valleys to forge, streams and deserts to cross. All these and many more will ultimately bring you closer to God.

I hope you use these situations as stepping-stones. Ask yourself, what is God trying to teach me? In every disaster, in victory and triumph, God will test you. He wants to see our reaction the moment something happens. Do you take the time to look to Him for the answers, or do you try to figure it all out yourselves?

I am here to say that my God is bigger than any problem I have; I'm not going to worry or fret. He has the power and I have the faith to claim my victory because that's the kind of God I serve! That may not comfort the lost, but as Christians we must hold our banner high so they can watch us overcome, receive the victory, and give God the glory.

CHAPTER 14

OBEDIENCE

Obedience is the first step in helping us to grow closer to God. With every obedient step we take, we are one step closer to God. When we ask Jesus into our hearts, we must submit our lives to the Father's will. In the book I'm reading by John Bevere, *Undercover*, obedience is not an option. Our first step is to be submitted to God, and seekers seek the will of God; to love Him is to obey Him. God doesn't have to demand obedience. It is because I love Him that I am hurt and ashamed when I disappoint Him.

I cry in repentance of my sin. Outwardly, people may see the tears and ask, "What is wrong?" I'm being cleansed from within. No matter how it seems, it is a good thing. Days and often weeks go by while I'm blinded by the sin in my life. Daily I need to ask Him to forgive me. When I have sin hidden in my life and it is revealed, I cry out to Him. God loves me and at the same time hates the sin in which I'm involved.

Pastor Carl said, "If you want to know how close you are to God, all you have to do is figure out how long it is from the time you sin until you ask for forgiveness." How quickly we acknowledge our sin and ask God to forgive us may be a good way to gauge how close we are to Him. God is awesome! He loves mankind more than we could even imagine. God is love and if we are to reflect Him then our lives must reflect His Love. God is love and the two are inseparable.

Have you ever been lost? I think all of us have been at some time in our lives. If we are driving in our car we can find someone and ask for directions. All alone and lost in the woods is quite different. That is where I am right now. After almost falling into the water, I'm going to move as God moves me. Right now I'm waiting for God to direct my steps through the dense thick trees. I've learned what could happen when I decide the direction in which I want my life to go. My life depends on seeking God's direction to find my way.

God will show me what to do. He will give me an inner sense of peace even when it is too loud for me to hear His voice. I know that in Psalms 54:7, the *Bible* states that, "God has rescued me from all my trouble, and triumphed over my enemies." Yet, I'm not afraid of failure. (The Living Bible)

Sometimes it seems that we fall down and get up on our own strength. Yet, I have learned that if we try on our own power nothing will go well. We need the power of the Holy Spirit that lives inside all of us who love the Lord. He will lead us if we continue to praise Him and look to heaven for the answers.

I want to get it right the first time, so I don't have to keep going round and round in circles, getting nowhere until I learn the lesson. God has everything all mapped out. I need His instruction. Progress for me is very slow at times because I'm not perfect and change is hard. I'm in constant battle with the enemy. Close to the finish line the devil lurks, waiting to trip me up. When my life gets rough, I know where I need to be.

Sometimes I feel so isolated and I have since learned that God didn't move. He still remained just as close as ever and still loves me. Yet, I was the one who felt abandoned. If you are standing facing someone and you turn around the opposite direction, you can't see them. They are out of sight because you are looking the wrong direction. I turned away from God; I couldn't see or feel Him in my life. We can't rely on our emotions and feelings. My life reflected a need that couldn't be met until I returned to God.

Commitment means to trust to another's care. Being committed means placing ourselves in the Master's care. My heart wasn't always totally committed to God. I wanted to be His but didn't fear disobeying Him. Pleasing God was not my heart's desire. All this led to the place I was when I thought God had abandoned me. I even prayed, "If there is anything I have done, please forgive me." Clueless, I went right on sinning by ignoring God's will for my life. I believe that we know better not to disappoint our bosses and we try hard to please our spouses. Isn't God more important? Yes we all know that He is!

While sitting in the woods, I learned quickly that God is my only lifeline. I'm unable to rescue myself. Jesus offers us a brand-new life! Born again, we begin living for God and to serve Him. We hold on to that new life, knowing it offers us more than our past existence. I'd like to say that the transformation in a new Christian's life instantly sheds them of their old way of doing things. But for most of us it is a relearning experience that takes a lifetime. God is still at work in me. I must hold on to my new life in Christ at all costs.

Getting lost and not finding Him could cost me my life. Worse yet is being lost and not even noticing. The lost I'm referring to are those who haven't found Jesus, who haven't asked Him to be their Lord and personal Savior. When we lose sight of God, we have lost our personal relationship with Him and our direction. It is sort of like being all alone and lost in the woods. Our survival depends on seeking and finding the Lord.

Psalm 91 says, "We live within the shadow of the Almighty,"... You have to be very close to Him to be in His shadow.

The rest of the verse states, "sheltered by the God who is above all gods." God will take care of us provided we don't allow other gods to come between us. We can't be sheltered unless we are so close that nothing comes between us. When things aren't going very well for us, God will defend us! He'll take the heat intended for us.

Seekers seek the direction of God. God loves us so much that even when we're lost, He shows us the right way to go. I have learned to walk by faith. I didn't get it right at first; I tried to carry the weight of all these struggles within me. Quickly getting lost in life's problems became so easy for me. Just a few steps into the woods and you're on your way.

Because sin can go to the core of a person, the roots have to be pulled out. I've slipped into the quicksand of sin and can't shake myself free. I am going under. Suddenly, God pulled me free from the sin in which I was engulfed. My heart was ready for the healing touch of the Master. I began seeking God and waiting for Him to transform me. If the sin had been a matter of changing my will I could've handled that. If I had needed more willpower the battle of sin could have been fought and won. But, this battle involved excess baggage from my past.

Obedience or having a submitted heart is the first step in allowing us to grow closer to God. With every obedient step we take, we are one step closer to God. When we ask Jesus into our hearts, we must submit our lives to the Father's will. Our love for God makes it easy to obey.

Obedience is number one and prayer is number two. Is there anyone in your life that you have a close relationship with that you don't communicate with? I believe it is impossible to be close to God by refusing to talk to Him. Prayer is not the only time each day when we can communicate with God. He is always listening and available 24/7.

CHAPTER 15

PRAYER

Finding a place to rest, I get down on my knees to talk to God.

Prayer is the one time each day when we know we have God's attention. He can communicate His plans to us. Remember to be still, quietly listening for His voice. I always think of prayer as my talking to God. All of us know what a compulsive talker is. We can barely say anything; they are doing all the talking. Don't we treat God the same way at times? We pray then close with an amen quickly getting back to business as usual. We should pray and then stop to listen.

Prayer is our personal time with God, when the Holy Spirit can communicate to us God's agenda for our day. Praying through out the day is also vitally important. Because if we don't seek or actually refuse to listen, we will miss the divine appointments for cultivating His love everywhere He sends us. We should pray and then stop to listen. How many of us buy something that requires assembling and proceed without reading the directions? Be still, quietly listening for His voice.

Prayer needs to be a more than a one-way communication, by talking to God and listening as God talks to us it allows us to make the right decisions about things that will happen through out our day. Now that's not the only way we can hear from God. Many people read the Bible and use it to hear from God. Praying and reading God's word go hand and hand and are essential to every believer. Yet it's easier for us to hear when we are focusing on Him before the distractions of this world start begging for our attention. We all need some quiet time reserved for God.

You might think there aren't enough hours in a day. Thinking that maybe I'll pray later if I find the time. That can lead us into disobedience and my will instead of surrendering to His. We all have the same amount of time every day. God gives it to us as a gift. How little or how much time you use to prepare yourself for the day depends on the individual. I have heard it said that if you skip praying, it will take you longer to finish your work. That is true if we are deciding what we need to do. When God is in charge, what we need to accomplish gets done. But worse than that is not knowing whose power is working in and for us. God's plan will help us avoid disaster.

After my mother died, we were traveling through the mountains on the way to her funeral. My daughter Stacy and I were busy chatting back and forth, while she was driving. My husband was in our van following behind us. All of a sudden my daughter hollered, "Look!" The driver right in front of us had lost control of his vehicle right after a car that was passing his car bumped him in on the rear end of the car. We watched as his vehicle veered off of the three lanes of traffic. He struggled to bring his car under control so he'd miss hitting the wooded area to the left of the interstate. Then as he lost total control of the car he was now heading right in front of us on just two wheels and was gliding back across the three lanes of heavy traffic. My daughter wanted to apply the brakes but knew if she did her dad, who was driving and was right behind us, would plow into us. She said, "I'm afraid to put on my brakes." I had begun praying the very moment the accident was happening. I was very specific: "Please, God, don't let us hit that car." I held my arm out. Then, I prayed that we wouldn't get hit in the rear. "God, please don't let anyone get hurt in this accident." The car made it across the three lanes and we watched as he left the highway, flipping over four times in the ravine to the right of the highway before landing right-side up. "Oh Lord," I cried, "please, don't let the man be injured." We stopped to assist the driver of course. Others also stopped to help except the person who had bumped him.

Miracle #1

The man walked around after getting out of the crumbled car.
He was walking around telling everyone that he was okay.

Miracle #2

Only one car was involved in the accident

Praying became instinctive; as soon as I saw the accident unfolding right before my eyes I began praying. Prayers went before us and through out the event. I believe that God intervened on our behalf and that only one car was involved because of answered prayer. What if I had not prayed immediately? We were following God and we are part of His plan.

That day, when we stopped to eat lunch we had prayed for traveling safety. I also prayed as the accident was unfolding before our eyes. Disaster was diverted because we took the time to pray. I shudder to think what could have happened if we had set out on our long trip without praying. On my adventure each morning, I pray and also as the day unfolds. Sometimes I ask God for a specific need. Many times in my thought life I have a conversation with God.

In the past, I have been driving along when the Holy Spirit has warned me to slow down. It wasn't because I was speeding. I obeyed and minutes later, a car would pull out in front of me. Once on the way to school, in the densest fog I had ever seen, I could barely see the road. It was the kind of conditions you would never drive in unless you had to be somewhere. I was trying hard to keep focused when I remembered that I had forgotten to take my pills that morning.

As it dawned on me, I said out loud, "Oh my, I forgot." Just then I took my foot off of the gas pedal. At that exact second a huge deer just jumped out nowhere or so it seemed right in front of my car. Missing it was incredible! I realized that slowing down those few seconds before had allowed the deer to make it to the other side of the road. Missing him was the Lord's intervening on my behalf. Forgetting to take my medication seemed like a bad thing. But the Lord allowed the memory of it to be used to save me from another accident.

Prayer is also the time to listen for God to speak. Sometimes we can hear His voice and other times He gives us such a peace about a specific situation. Now exactly what does God want us to do? Seek Him always and continually as we enjoy our lives. That is why prayer and reading the Bible are essential in drawing us to a closer walk with God. God wants you to talk to Him and His desire is to satisfy you with everything you need. So be still and quietly listen for His voice.

1. Pray.
2. Read the Bible.
3. Seek to do God's will.
4. Get hungry for more of God.

How, you may ask? First you should begin by putting your priorities in order. On this journey I'd be lost without the assistance from the Holy Spirit. The adventure is exciting when I'm guided to new places and sometimes I'm totally unaware of my mission. Life gets dangerous when I set out on my own. Disasters await us and nothing is going to happen to us that God isn't already aware of. Anything we are facing is never too big for us to handle with the help of the Holy Spirit.

By praying and reading God's word each morning, I have started my day off right. With God's help we can walk in the spirit and not in the flesh. We can gain insight and wisdom to guide us through each day. I used to think of prayer as just my talking to God. But I have learned that it is a two-way conversation. Each day we must ask God for His help to be submitted to Him.

Well, I'm done praying and the Holy Spirit is guiding me through these dense woods. I'm sure glad I'm not trying to navigate my way on my own. The woods are thick and the going is slow. Oh, great; I hear rippling water. There must be a stream up ahead. There is a gentle breeze and the leaves make a rhapsody of music with their clapping sound. In the distance I see water flowing into a plush green mossy brook. It is a not only a spectacular sight but also a refreshing one. Water! Traveling through these woods is tiring. I get so hot and thirsty; the journey seems slow. Yet, I have been brought to this water for more than the calm and peaceful atmosphere.

In Acts 3:19 the word of God speaks about repenting, having your sins blotted out, so that times of refreshing will come from the presence of the Lord. I believe it is impossible to have a close relationship with God without feeling His presence.

If the water in this stream symbolizes my walk with God, think about this: The deeper I press in living a Bible centered life, the more the word of God will refresh me. When I am in the water ankle deep my feet benefit, but the rest of my body is still hot. The deeper I submerge my body into the water, the more refreshed I'll become.

God will pour out Himself to the level that we seek Him. On this journey to eternity, I believe that you only get what you're willing to strive for. We must get hungry for more of God. The more time I spend thinking about God, the more joy and peace I have inside. "Now may the Lord of peace Himself give you peace always and in every way." (2 Thessalonians 3:16)

May the joy of the Lord be your strength. Joy comes from standing in faith on the word of God. I can read scriptures and they will minister strength to my physical and emotional needs. Yet, it is the planting of the word on the inside of me that I need more of. How do we plant God's word in our hearts and minds to activate His potential for us? Impartation begins the moment the scriptures intertwine around our hearts and become an integral part of who we are. When we think and act as the words activate us we will be transformed.

Let me use the example of a glass of water. We all know that by drinking the water, it gets on the inside of us. Let's say the water represents the living water. We can meditate on one scripture. During the day, if the scripture comes to your mind, then the word refreshes you and gives you precisely just what you need at that very moment.

We stand on the word of God when we believe it to be true and live our lives in obedience to God. As humans we are taught to think. Yet as a born-again Christians we must not rely on our own understanding, because God may call us to do what seems illogical and impossible. Convenient is not in God's vocabulary, many times we will be asked to do things when we least expect it. Daily I must listen to the Holy Spirit as He instructs, teaches, and guides me.

While on my spiritual journey, I realize that God has allowed me to drag my sins around literally so that I could see them. I don't have to look inside at all these burdens because I feel the weight of my sin. If I jumped into the water right now I might drown. So as I kneel to pray I also reach inside and pull out all of my sins the greed, idolatry, lust, and gossip.

Repenting is my first step into the water. As I repent for my sins I am drawn closer and closer to the Lamb of God. We are designed to get all our needs met by God and to be drawn to Him. When I take a drink of water, it does no more than quench my thirst. It is God that sustains my life. We can't live without the living water. We can, however, live a short time without food. I had several packs of cheese and crackers, four candy bars, and a package of beef jerky. Yet, it has been days since I've eaten anything. I'm not taking another step until I find something to eat.

According to Pastor Chip Judd, idolatry is attempting to use anyone or anything to meet a need in your life that only God can meet. We go on vacations to relax and get revived. Have you ever returned home tired and exhausted? Do we need a vacation from our vacation? No, not really. Yet, we want to receive tranquility. Only the Lord can truly immerse us in it as we come into His presence.

STRENGTH FROM THE BIBLE

The Lord's power will sustain us where nothing else can! The Bible is one of our greatest weapons of warfare inside of us waiting for us to activate it. Deep within us faith rises up from meditating on His word, the Bible. Faith believes God for the impossible and our faith grows stronger by hearing, receiving and believing what the word of God states about our circumstances.

Reading the Bible is essential for the transformation of our spirit man, as food is to fuel to our physical bodies; without both we can't live successful lives. If water represents Jesus, then I will use food to symbolize His word. Just looking at food will not benefit us, it isn't until we eat or until we put it inside us, where our bodies can draw strength from its nutrients. How do we plant the word of God in our hearts? We meditate on it day and night, until the scripture comes to our minds when we need it. By putting it on the inside of us, we gain the wisdom needed to walk in righteousness, standing right with God doing what He wants us to do at that precise moment.

Just as I have to get into the water to get refreshed, drinking the living water quenches the inside of me in a way that just casually looking at it won't. Well, the word of God is the same way. We need to get closer than just looking at it. We have to consume scriptures until they are planted on the inside. When your thoughts become strengthened by the written word that ministers to you long after you have read it, you're there.

I think I'll sit down right now and meditate on the word of God.

Psalm 91

He who dwells in the secret place of the Most High
Shall abide under the shadow of the Almighty.
I will say of the Lord, "He is my refuge and my fortress;
My God, in Him I will trust."

Surely He shall deliver you from the snare of the fowler
And from the perilous pestilence.
He shall cover you with His feathers,
And under His wings you shall take refuge;

His truth shall be your shield and buckler.
You shall not be afraid of the terror by night,
Nor of the arrow that flies by day,
Nor of the pestilence that walks in darkness,
Nor of the destruction that lays waste at noonday.

A thousand may fall at your side,
And ten thousand at your right hand;
But it shall not come near you.
Only with your eyes shall you look,
And see the reward of the wicked.

Because you have made the Lord, who is my refuge,
Even the Most High, your dwelling place,
No evil shall befall you,
Nor shall any plague come near your dwelling;
For He shall give His angels charge over you,
To keep you in all your ways.
In their hands they shall bear you up,
Lest you dash your foot against a stone.
You shall tread upon the lion and the cobra,
The young lion and the serpent you shall trample
underfoot.

Because he has set his love upon Me, therefore I will
deliver him;
I will set him on high, because he has known My name.
He shall call upon Me and I will answer him;
I will be with him in trouble;
I will deliver him and honor him.
With long life I will satisfy him,
And show him My salvation."

In His arms, we are safe. Under His wings, you will find refuge. In His presence comes healing, joy, and peace. We are safe from the enemy. True obedience grants us many benefits. God loves to bless His children. On the other side of the brook was a lush green meadow where I laid down in the green grass to rest. It is one of those places you just wish you could stay forever.

On school days, we take our four children to school each morning. If they rode the bus in the morning they would have to get up too early. The pickup time is around six a.m. On most afternoons, they ride the bus home from school.

On this particular afternoon, Michael was going to the library. I expected the girls to come home on the bus. When Sarah came in the door, she asked, "Why did you come and pick up Betty from school?" I quickly stated, "I didn't pick Betty up!" "She wasn't on the bus?" I asked.

I called the school but there was no answer. School had been dismissed two hours earlier. Everyone had probably already gone home. How would I find out what happened to my daughter? I had no idea where she was. Immediately I prayed for her protection and placed guardian angels around her to keep her safe. I also prayed that she wouldn't be afraid. I didn't panic because of my faith in God.

In fifteen minutes my husband would be home from work. I was sure he would know what to do. So Sarah and I waited. Ray was very shocked when I told him that Rebecca hadn't gotten off the bus. He quickly placed a call to the bus superintendent. We all stood there gazing at each other, not knowing what to think. Could she have gotten on the wrong bus?

Rebecca's teacher lived only a mile from us. I drove there to ask her what could have possibly gone wrong. There was no one home. When I was walking back into our house the phone was ringing. The school's janitor had found her. Earlier that day, all the children

94

in her class were lying on the kindergarten floor for their naps. Rebecca had been talking so much that she was moved to the very back of the room behind a desk that had a computer setting on it. She is a very sound sleeper and had a bad cold that afternoon. She slept through all the dismissal bells and went unnoticed by her two teachers.

Soon she was on her way home and back into our arms again. She was still groggy from such a long nap. The principal apologized, saying how sorry she was. We were so happy to have her safely back home again. Later that evening her teacher called to ask us to forgive her. I told her it was all right, Rebecca was fine.

She was very surprised that I wasn't mad at her and was very calm. The answer is really quite easy. I was ready for that storm because of my close walk with the Lord. My faith and confidence were all I needed. I had prayed, placing Rebecca in God's care, and it was all I needed to be at peace. No matter what the outcome was, Jesus would be there for me. I placed my trust in God and that gave me my faith, not fear. The definition our pastor gives for fear is:

False
Evidence
Appearing
Real

I knew Rebecca was missing but also that everything was still in God's hands. So I put my faith in God, who will always be there to help us make it through every storm. Rebecca tells the story much differently. She remembers waking up and wondering where all the people were. I asked her if she was afraid. She stated, "No." She left the room looking for someone and found the janitor. I bet he was surprised upon discovering a student hours after school was over.

I was not in control. God was in control! So I didn't need to panic or worry. The first thing I did was pray. I relied on my faith in God to get me through and He did. The storm came without warning; I had no idea where Rebecca was. We must stay prepared. God is always in control of every situation. How much we depend on Him is up to us. The Lord's power is always inside of us waiting for us to activate it.

The lesson I've learned is to follow in His footsteps no matter where He's leading me. Sometimes I'm at the end of a rope, wondering how God is going to save me. I would prefer to know exactly what is going to happen next. Even in all my planning the events of my day almost always turn out differently than I ever imagined. Excellence is when everything goes according to His plan.

I'm blind and don't know where God will lead me. It's dangerous when I do know my destination especially when I think I'm in charge. With God, I don't always know where I'm going. Yet I thank the Lord for that! It's a moment-to-moment experience that is exhilarating.

CHAPTER 16

IN HIS PRESENCE

What is the one quality that every believer has that sets him apart from the crowd? I am sure everyone could name several things. Excitement for life is one quality that I think everyone wants for their lives, whether they are saved or not. We are all blessed, yet, it is those who radiate God's love by always having a smile on their faces and a special glow from being in His presence that stand out.

They are bubbling over with joy and such happiness that spills over into their conversations. That they just can't wait to talk about what wonderful things God is up to in their lives. They know how blessed they are. We like to hang around those kinds of people, hoping some of what they have will rub off on us. It is the joy of the Lord that becomes their strength in all circumstances.

Children often have this sunny outlook. My five-year-old looks at a full moon and calls it a "whole moon." When the weather outside causes the lights to flicker in our home. Rebecca says the lights are blinking because they are sleepy. She delights in the smallest of things: that astounds me. If only I could see the world through her eyes.

She had three days off from school. I asked her what she would like to do. She gleamed with delight as a picnic was planned as our special thing to do together. When I said we would have time to do one more thing. Her response was that we could have two picnics. We had our feast outside on that beautify spring day.

I'm thinking, what is the big deal? We're just eating outside. We did use doll-size dishes. It was nice! My daughter thought it was spectacular. She was so excited about Mommy and her tea party. The world seems to change from a different viewpoint. To a small child even the smallest of things can be special. Children love spending time with their parents.

Just as children crave spending time with their parents we should also steal time away with our Heavenly Father. I used to find a quiet place to rest after supper. Alone with God I could share or just quietly listen. It was our time and nothing could take its place.

Our little six-year-old girl went to kiss her daddy. As he leaned down for the kiss, she threw her arms around his neck and wouldn't let go. He sat down so he could hold her in his arms. It's just like that with us. God gets so close we want to climb into His arms. In the presence of Jehovah, the cares of this world melt away. He can't resist holding us, His children.

That's as close as we can get. God is always waiting for us to climb in His arms. In His presence is the ultimate place to be. That's where I want to stay. Do you want to get into His presence? Then stop right now and spend some quiet time ….

In the spirit world I'm soaring like an eagle, so excited about my next assignment! At the very top of the mountain I look and as far as my eyes can see I know I could be literally going to the other side of the world. The decisions we make while seeking God's will for our lives will take us on one of the greatest spiritual adventures of all times, and that is how our new journey begins. ...

CPSIA information can be obtained
at www.ICGtesting.com
Printed in the USA
LVOW08s2049280217
525709LV00001B/5/P